I0125845

Richard Gilmour

The new third reader

Richard Gilmour

The new third reader

ISBN/EAN: 9783741156236

Manufactured in Europe, USA, Canada, Australia, Japa

Cover: Foto ©Thomas Meinert / pixelio.de

Manufactured and distributed by brebook publishing software
(www.brebook.com)

Richard Gilmour

The new third reader

THE CATHOLIC NATIONAL SERIES.

THE
NEW THIRD READER

BY

RT. REV. RICHARD GILMOUR, D.D.,
BISHOP OF CLEVELAND.

NEW YORK, CINCINNATI, AND CHICAGO:

BENZIGER BROTHERS,

PRINTERS TO THE HOLY APOSTOLIC SEE.

HARVARD COLLEGE LIBRARY
GIFT OF THE
GRADUATE SCHOOL OF EDUCATION

15 May 29

Copyright, 1891, by BENZIGER BROTHERS.

CONTENTS.

viii CONTENTS.

Lessons marked with an asterisk (*) are adapted from "The Ave Maria."

PUNCTUATION.

The *Comma* (,), *Semicolon* (;), and *Colon* (:) are used to separate the parts of a long sentence ; as, *Charles, my youngest brother, has gone to the city ; as he was leaving, I said to him : Write to me as soon as you arrive.*

The *Period* (.) is used at the end of a complete declarative sentence. It is also used to mark an abbreviation ; as, *Right Rev. Dr. John Carroll was the first bishop of the United States.*

The *Interrogation Point* (?) is used after a question ; as, *How do you do?*

The *Exclamation Point* (!) is used after an exclamation ; as, *O, dear ! why did you show me that ?*

The *Dash* (—) is used to show a sudden turn in the thought ; as, *No one cares for the fortress — that can go.*

The *Apostrophe* (') is used to show that one or more letters of a word have been omitted, and also to denote ownership ; as, *In ev'ry tongue. The boy's hat.*

The *Hyphen* (-) is used to connect the parts of a compound word ; as, *All-souls'-day.* When placed at the end of a line, the *hyphen* shows that one or more syllables of a word are carried forward to the next line. It is also used where a word is divided into syllables ; as, *Dif-fi-cul-ty.*

The *Quotation Marks* (" ") are used to show that the words which they enclose are taken from another author or speaker ; as, *God says : "Honor your father and your mother."*

The *Parenthesis* (( )) is used to enclose a word or sentence inserted by way of explanation ; as, *The story of "Jack's Wood Pile" (beginning on page 137) is very interesting.*

PHONIC MARKS USED IN THIS READER.

VOWELS.

ā, long, *as in* dāy

ă, short, *as in* făn

â *as in* beâr

ä, Italian, *as in* cärt

à *as in* àsk

ą, broad, *as in* bąll .

ạ, *like short* ŏ, *as in* whạt

ē, long, *as in* bē

ĕ, short, *as in* pĕn

ê, *like* â, *as in* thêir

ẹ, *like long* ā, *as in* obẹy

ē̄ *as in* lēarn

ī, long, *as in* rīde

ĭ, short, *as in* sĭt

ï, *like long* ē, *as in* Zïta

ī̄, *like* ē̄, *as in* fīrm

ō, long, *as in* rōpe

ŏ, short, *as in* chŏp

ô, *like short* ŭ, *as in* dône

ǫ, *like long* o͞o, *as in* whǫ

ọ, *like short* o͝o, *as in* wọuld

ô, *like broad* ą, *as in* hôrse

o͞o, long, *as in* scho͞ol

o͝o, short, *as in* lo͝ok

ū, long, *as in* blūe

ŭ, short, *as in* bŭt

ụ, *preceded by* r, *as in* trụe

ụ, *like short* o͝o, *as in* pụt

û *as in* tûrn

ȳ, long, *as in* bȳ

y̆, short, *as in* dolly̆

ạ, ẹ, ị, ọ, ụ, *have an obscure sound similar to that of short* ŭ.

à, ẹ̀, ò, *are similar in sound to long* ā, ē, ō, *but are not to be pronounced so long.*

CONSONANTS.

ç, soft, *like* s *sharp, as in* çent

c, hard, *like* k, *as in* call

ġ, hard, *as in* ġave

ġ, soft, *like* j, *as in* stranġe

ṣ, soft, *like* z., *as in* haṣ

th, flat, *as in* then

n *as in* uncle

SUGGESTIONS TO TEACHERS.

The object of the following suggestions is to assist overworked teachers, by showing partly how this book *may* be used.

As we can not read correctly unless we understand the meaning of every word, it is important that pupils should master the *vocabularies* that precede the lessons. The meaning of the words may be inferred from the context, but to make sure that they are properly understood, the pupils may be asked to construct sentences with them. Besides defining these words, the pupils ought to spell them orally, either by the phonic or the alphabetic method, but they should never be allowed to spell while reading. Afterward, however spelled, the words should be copied, care being taken that they are correctly syllabified and accented, and that the proper diacritical marks are employed. Familiarity with these marks soon enables pupils to pronounce new words without assistance.

The exercises that follow the lessons should never be neglected, as they help to familiarize the pupils with our language. They embrace

Language Lessons, which comprise

Questions on the topics treated in the lesson; Dictation Exercises, wherein unfamiliar words are explained in short, easy sentences, and by the help of synonyms; suggestions for the explanation of difficult phrases and sentences; changing word-forms, by means of affixes, and by the formation of plurals; changing verse into prose; homophonous words, presented, for the most part, in simple sentences; drill on words frequently mispro-

nounced by misplacing the accent, misusing the
elementary sounds, or by wrong syllabification;
Exercises in Articulation, an excellent practice in
the pronunciation of the various elementary
sounds and their combinations; Familiar Talks on
Common Things, which serve not only to convey
useful and valuable information, but provide am-
ple material for composition and for dictation.
In every exercise, but especially in composition,
attention must be given to the proper use of
capital letters and punctuation marks.

Pupils should be required to read in a natural
tone and without affectation. The pitch should
be neither too soft nor too loud, and the reading
should show intelligence and interest.

Questions, varying as much as possible in form,
should be asked about each part of a lesson, and
proper answers in complete sentences secured
from the pupils.

The light and attractive "conversational" style,
which has proved so popular in our *New Second
Reader*, has been, in a great measure, followed in
this Reader.

The subject-matter of the lessons has been
so chosen that it may interest and instruct. There
are but few "religious" lessons, but there is an un-
mistakable Catholic tone on every page, which
shows that the book is intended for Catholic
schools only.

The illustrations have been made for the lessons. They are the work of excellent artists, and
are all that taste, skill, and money can make them.

The book is presented in the hope that it will
prove as acceptable and popular as the other books
of the series, and that it will find a lasting place
in Catholic schools.

THIRD READER

LESSON I.

măĭd	băk'er	bŭtch'er	pōŭlt'rў
stŭffs	tăn'ner	mā'sǫns	‑eär'pen-terş
tāĭ'lor	bŭt'tǫn	wĕăv'ing	sŭg'ar-‑eānĕ

Dictation Exercise.

I like chickens and ducks better than any other kind of *poultry*, but John likes turkeys and geese.

Grace's Servants.

1. "Dear me! I can not button my shoe," said Grace, "and no one offers to help me. I wish I were like cousin Ellen, who has a maid to tend to her. I have no one to wait on me."

2. "No one to wait on you!" said her mother. "Why, how can you say that, my child? There are thousands waiting on you. There is the farmer,

for you, and sends you butter, milk, cheese, eggs, and poultry. The baker makes bread for you, and the butcher supplies you with meat.

3. "Then there are people in different parts of the world, men, women, and children, who are busy weaving cotton, wool, and silk for your use; and the tailor and dressmaker, who make up these stuffs into clothes for ‘ you. Besides, there is the tanner, who dresses leather, and the shoemaker, who makes it into shoes and slippers.

4. "Just think, too, of the people who are picking tea for you to drink, and of others who are gathering coffee for you. What would you do for sweet-meats or cake, if there were no one cutting down sugar-cane that you may have sugar?

5. "There are carpenters and masons, and painters, too, and ever so many other people, more than I could think of in an hour, all working that you may be happy and comfortable. No one to wait on you! Never say that again, my child."

Language Lesson.

Let the answers to the following questions be in complete sentences.

1. Who raises grain, vegetables, and fruit for us?
2. Who sends us butter, milk, cheese, and eggs?
3. Who makes bread for us?
4. Who supplies us with meat?
5. What does the tanner do?
6. What is meant by *poultry?*

Let the pupils select and write from the lesson a statement, a question, and an exclamation, like the following example:

Statement.—I have no one to wait on me.
Question.—Have I no one to wait on me?
Exclamation.—No one to wait on me!

Proverb.

To be copied and learned by heart.

A good name is better than riches.

LESSON II.

lănǩ   Běs'sў   rěd'děn
South   Frěd'dў   seăm'per

What the Winds Bring.

1. Which is the wind that brings the cold?
The North wind, Freddy, and all the snow.
And the sheep will scamper into the fold,
When the North begins to blow.

2. Which is the wind that brings the heat?

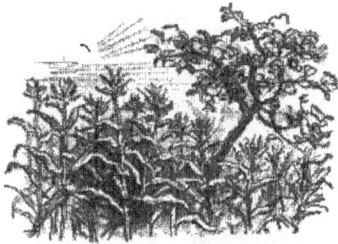

The South wind, Katie; and corn will grow,
And peaches redden for you to eat,
When the South begins to blow.

3. Which is the wind that brings the rain?

The East wind, Willy;
and farmers know
That cows come shivering up the lane,
When the East begins to blow.

4. Which is the wind that brings the flowers?

The West wind, Bessy; and soft and low
The birdies sing in the summer hours,
When the West begins to blow.

Language Lesson.

Let the pupils change the verses into prose, and make the statements in their own language, orally in class, and as a written exercise at home. The written home exercise will prove useful for supplementary reading.

What word rhymes with *cold?* With *snow?* With *heat?* With *rain?* With *flowers?*

LESSON III.

whạrf	kĭt′tᴇ̨ns	mọvᴇ̨′ment
ŏt′ter	găm′bolș	a-void′ing
se-lĕet′	lŏ′eusts	to-bŏg′gan
sĭg′nal	elĭʀ̨k′ing	A-mĕr′i-eạ

The Plays of Animals.

1. People who take the trouble to watch and study animals and their ways, know that they have their games and plays which they enjoy greatly.

2. A gentleman, who lived in South America, tells how he watched daily from an old wharf a school of fishes playing what looked very much like a game of tag. The water under the wharf was perfectly clear, and as the bed of the river was of pure, silvery sand, every movement of the fishes could be seen. One little fish would dart at another, and then would be joined by the rest; they all would follow the leader, chasing him round the piles and posts. After a while, they would turn and chase some other fish till it was "tagged."

to enjoy most was that of jumping. The jumping was not under water, but was done in this way: As the tide rose, it carried out many sticks that had been thrown on the shore. As soon as the fishes saw a stick, a number of them would dart at it, and with a flirt of their tails, a splash and a clatter, over they would go, out of the water, clearing the stick. This play would sometimes continue for hours, and often a number of these games would be going on at once.

4. At another time, the same gentleman, when in the country, saw six or eight large locusts, commonly called grasshoppers, hopping about, hiding behind stones, and showing great cunning in avoiding one another. Their movements were very much like those of a cat, they were so sly.

5. When the locusts were tired of playing hide-and-seek, they began a jumping game. Two would face, and spring into the air, one leaping over the other; then they would turn about and repeat the game. At the same

time they made a clicking sound, as
if it were a signal to begin or end
the play.

6. A very learned man used to say
that the toboggan was probably sug-

gested by seeing otters at play. Otters
have their home in the neighborhood of
a stream; they build their nests in the
bank, and have, generally, one entrance
in the water and another on shore.
During the winter, these animals select
a steep bank that leads into the water
or out upon the ice. On this the snow

is carefully patted down and made smooth, till it is a bed of ice. This done, the otters start at the top of the hill, and away they go dashing down, either to splash into the water or slide over the ice. The animals keep up this for a long time, and hunters watch the slides, as they are sure always to find otters there.

7. The sun bear will play for hours with a ball or a log of wood. The common black bear is almost as playful, and its rough-and-tumble games are most interesting to watch.

8. We have all seen the cat play with her kittens, and have watched the gambols of the pet dog. Thus animals, large and small, even the tiny insects, have their games and sports.

Language Lesson.

Let the answers be in complete sentences.

1. Where is South America?
2. What is a *wharf?*
3. How did the fishes play *tag?*
4. How did they jump?
5. How did the locusts play?
6. What is said to have suggested the toboggan?
7. What is meant by the *gambols* of the pet dog?

LESSON IV.

loud	trṳ'lў	As-sï'ṣï	Ăn'tḣo-nў
wĕpt	shōẉn	Bĕr'nard	pär'tridgҽ
pō'et	hĕȧlҽd	de Sālҽṣ	per-mĭs'sion
dŭmҍ	Jĕr'ọmҽ	spăr'rōẉṣ	re-märk'a-blҽ

Our Dumb Friends.

1. The holy ones of the earth have always shown a great love and tenderness for dumb creatures.

2. St. Anthony preached to the fishes; St. Jerome healed a sick lion; St. John cared for a pet partridge; St. Bernard loved to free birds from the traps set for them; and St. Francis de Sales wept with joy to see some doves share a meal with sparrows.

3. The gentleness of St. Francis of Assisi toward dumb animals was remarkable. The birds of the air and the beasts of the field and forest he called his brothers and sisters, "for," said he, "our dear Lord is their Father as well as mine."

4. He often spoke to the birds as

much to God, your Creator, and you
ought to sing His praises at all times.
Study always to praise the Lord."

5. The birds would not fly away when
he went near them, but would continue

to sing so loud, that at times the monks
who were with the Saint could not hear
one another speak.   But when Francis
bade them stop singing, the birds at
once obeyed, nor would they begin
again, till the Saint gave them permis-

6. Let us never be ashamed to be kind and gentle to the meanest of God's creatures. A great poet has truly said :

He prayeth best who loveth best
　All things both great and small;
For the dear God who loveth us
　He made and loveth all.

Language Lesson.

Let the answers be in complete sentences.

1. Who preached to the fishes?
2. Who healed a sick lion?
3. What did St. John care for?
4. What did St. Bernard love to do?
5. What made St. Francis de Sales weep?
6. What do you understand by the expression *dumb creatures,* in paragraph 1?

Let the pupils learn by heart what the poet has said.

Exercises In Articulation.

Drill the pupils in pronouncing the d in these words :

old	lived	build	tired
bed	looked	sound	round
and	joined	found	seemed

Let the pupils double the last letter in each of the following words and add ing.

LESSON V.

ġĕmṣ	çĕn'ter	mis-lĕd'	mĭll'ionṣ
trãçẹ	vĭs'ion	sĭm'plẹ	(mĭl'yuns)
drạwn	(vĭsh'un)	dĭs'tant	hōmẹ'ward
shōnẹ	sue-çĕsṣ'	spärk'lẹ	dis-mĭsṣẹd'
whĕnçẹ	bĭd'dẹn	sĕrv'ant	ɛon-fīd'ed
Mĕx'i-ɛan		dĭs-ap-pĕạrẹd'	

Dictation Exercise.

In the king's crown were diamonds, emeralds, and
other *gems*.

A Mexican Legend.

1. In the early part of December, in
the year 1531, a poor Mexican Indian,
named John, left the little village where
he lived to go to the city of Mexico,
about three miles distant. He started
before daybreak, for he wanted to be
in time to hear Mass in honor of the
Blessed Virgin, for whom he had great
devotion.

2. Day was beginning to break as
John reached the foot of a mountain,
which he was just about to climb,
when he heard the sound of music.
Looking up to find whence it came, he
saw a bright, white cloud. From the.

center of this cloud shone a ray of light, forming a halo in which were all the colors of the rainbow.

3. John could scarcely believe his eyes, till he heard a sweet voice call his name. He hastened to climb the hill, and at the top found a very beautiful woman, around whom shone a light that made the stones and bushes sparkle like gems.

4. When the Indian had drawn near, our Blessed Lady, for it was she, told him that she wished a church to be built on that spot, and bade him go to Mexico and tell this to the bishop.

5. On reaching the city, John went straight to the bishop, and humbly related what the Blessed Virgin had confided to him. The bishop listened with attention, but fearing John might be misled, he put him off, and bade him come again.

6. John returned homeward, feeling very sad. When he reached the place of the vision, he saw our Blessed Mother waiting for him. He was not surprised,

feet, and told her of his want of success.

7. The Blessed Virgin listened with kindness, and told John she had millions of angels at her command, but she had chosen him, her faithful servant, for this work. She ordered him to return to the bishop and repeat the message. Poor John told her he was afraid it would be useless, but promised to obey.

8. He went to Mexico the next day, and, in his simple manner, told the bishop he had seen the Blessed Virgin a second time and she had again commanded him to have a church built in her honor.

9. "I believe you," said the bishop, "but to be still more certain, ask her who sends you for some sign by which we may know if she be really the Mother of God." The bishop then dismissed John, but sent some servants to follow him and note what happened.

10. The servants did as they were bidden, but suddenly the Indian disappeared, and no trace of him could be

found. Then the servants returned,
and told the bishop that John was de-
ceiving him, and ought to be punished.

Exercises In Articulation.

Drill the pupils in pronouncing the t in these words:

acts	coast	host	modest
best	dust	wept	swiftest

LESSON VI.

dew	it-sĕlf′	rĕl′a-tīvẹ
päth	ɇon-çĕạl′	sūit′a-blẹ
prōōf	de-ṣīrẹd′	at-tĕmpt′ed
queen	dis-ɇŏv′erẹd	sim-plĭç′i-tў
pär′dǫn	ɇon-fūṣẹd′	im-măɇ′u-lātẹ

A Mexican Legend—(*Continued*).

1. In the meantime, John went to
the spot where his Blessed Mother was
awaiting him. As before, he knelt at
her feet and repeated what the bishop
had said. With great tenderness our
Lady bade him come to her the next
day, saying she would give him the
sign for which the bishop asked.

2. John promised to return; but when
he reached home, he found his uncle
verv ill. He remained with the sick

man till the second day; then, as he grew worse, John started to bring a priest, so that his relative might receive the last Sacraments.

3. Remembering that he had not kept his promise, and fearing to meet the Blessed Virgin, the Indian took another path, and was hurrying on, when he saw her coming down the hill to meet him. "My son," said she, "where are you going?"

4. The Indian, confused, threw himself at the feet of his Queen, and said with simplicity, "Well-beloved Virgin, do not be displeased with me. I am going for a priest, that my uncle, your servant, who is dangerously ill, may make his confession and receive the last Sacraments. Pardon me, and I will return at daybreak to-morrow without fail."

5. When he had finished speaking, the Blessed Virgin told him that his uncle was cured. "Go now," she said, "to the top of the hill, and gather the roses that are blooming there. Put them in your cloak, and bring them to

me; I will tell you what to do with
them."

6. Though John believed there were
no roses there, he obeyed without a
word. How great,
then, was his
surprise
to find a
garden
rich

with flowers. Filling his cloak with
roses, he placed it on his shoulders, and
hurried back to his Queen.

7. Our Lady took the roses in her
pure hands, and letting them drop back
into the cloak, said to John, "Present
these to the bishop, and say that they

are the proof of the command I give
you. Do not show any one what you
carry, and open your cloak only in
the presence of the bishop."

8. Thanking the Blessed Virgin, John
started once more for the city. When
he reached the bishop's house, the servants noticed that he carried something
in his cloak which he wished to conceal,
and they began to push and pull the
poor Indian about, till they discovered
what he had. At sight of the roses, the
men attempted to take them from him,
but whenever they were touched they
turned to painted flowers on the Indian's cloak.

9. When John was brought before
the bishop, he opened his cloak to
show the sign that was to prove his
words, and fresh, sweet-smelling roses,
wet with dew, fell to the floor, while
on the cloak itself appeared a beautiful
picture of the Immaculate Mother of
God.

10. "The finger of God is here," said
the bishop, and then he knelt before
the picture, and gave praise to God.

The miraculous picture was placed in the principal church of Mexico, where it remained till a suitable chapel was built on the hill, as the Blessed Virgin desired.

Exercises in Articulation.

Drill the pupils in pronouncing th flat.

than	thine	breathe	mother
with	though	feather	wealthy

Drill the pupils, also, in pronouncing th sharp.

both	earth	thin	thank
south	month	three	thought

LESSON VII.

ġĭn	bûrsts	grōwth	băg'ġing
răgs	clŏth	pûr'plę	sọ̆ŭth'ern
frŏst	bālęs	clī'matę	ma-çhïnę'
çēạsę	stātęs	păd'ding	eẋ-ăm'plę
clŏth'ing	con-tāïn'ing		sĕp'a-rāt-ed

Dictation Exercise.

Peàs grow in a *pod.*—If your heart should *cease,* or stop, beating, you would die.—A goose is covered with soft, *downy* feathers.

Cotton.

1. "Grandmother," asked Ellen, "how is cotton made?"

"Made! my dear," answered grandma, "why, cotton grows. Not the sort of cotton you sew with, but the soft, downy kind that is used for padding. From this, cotton thread is spun.

2. "A field of cotton is a beautiful sight, either when covered with yellow and purple blossoms, or with the white cotton.

3. "The cotton plant grows only in a warm climate, as for example, in our southern states. When the blossom dies, it is followed by a pod containing a number of black seeds which lie in a bed of fine, soft cotton. When ripe, these pods break open, and the snow-white cotton bursts out in long curls.

4. "Then begins a busy time. All hands, young and old, are kept hard at work, from daylight till dark, picking the cotton. Nor does the work cease, till the first frost stops the growth of the plant.

5. "Afterward, the cotton is spread out to dry, and is then separated from the seeds. This was formerly done by hand, and took a long time, but now

the work is done better and more quickly by a machine called a cotton-gin.

6. "The seeds are not thrown away, for a valuable oil is pressed from them, and the mass that remains is used as food for cattle, which are very fond of it.

7. "The clean cotton is next packed in large bundles, called bales, which are covered with a coarse cloth, known as bagging; then it is ready to be sent

by boat or railroad to the mill. At the mill, the cotton is spun into thread, and this is made into many kinds of cloth. More than half of our clothing is made of cotton.

8. "O, I almost forgot to say," continued grandma, "that even when our clothes are worn out and in rags, the cotton is still of use, for these rags are sent to the paper-mill, and the best book-paper is made of them."

"O, thank you, grandmother," said Ellen. "How many things you re- . member!"

Language Lesson.

Let the answers be in complete sentences.

1. Of what is cotton made?
2. Where does cotton grow?
3. What follows when the cotton blossom dies?
4. When does "a busy time" begin in a cotton field?
5. What is done with the cotton when it is dry?
6. What use is made of the cotton seed?
7. When does the work of picking cotton cease?
8. How is the cotton separated from the seeds?
9. How is the clean cotton packed?
10. With what kind of cloth are the bales covered?
11. Of what is the greater part of our clothing made?
12. What is made of cotton rags?

LESSON VIII.

seōld	strōllĕd	dis-pĕrsĕd'
răs'eal	eås'soçk	mu-ṣĭ'çianṣ
elĕr'ġy̆	eăn'o-py̆	de-tĕet'ed
stāinĕd	sûr'plïçĕ	so-çī'e-tïĕṣ
bădġ'eṣ	stū'dents	ea-thĕ'dral
Ҫôr'pus Ҫhrīs'tï		gŏŏd-năt'urĕd-ly̆

Dictation Exercise.

I did not walk fast, but *strolled* down the road. —A
boy *detected* the thief as he was running off with
my coat. —The rain soon *dispersed* the crowd.

One Good Turn Deserves Another.

1. "Stop pushing, you little rascal,"
said a soldier who was standing near
the edge of the sidewalk to watch the
Corpus Christi procession.

2. "But I want to see," answered the
boy to whom he spoke. "I can hear the
music, but I cannot see a thing. The
procession is coming out of the cathedral, and I shall miss the sight. I wish
you would take me on your shoulders."

3. The soldier did not answer. Indeed, before he had time to say a word,
the boy had climbed up his back and

4. The crowd laughed, while the soldier good-naturedly allowed the boy to remain where he was.

5. The head of the procession was just in line with them. It was really a grand sight. First came the musicians; then the school children dressed in their best and wearing bright badges; next the college students and the different societies, carrying gay banners; then followed the clergy, and, under a canopy of white and gold silk, the Bishop bearing the Blessed Sacrament. Carrying the canopy were four of the leading men of the city, while after them marched a crowd of pious people.

6. "O, how beautiful, how beautiful!" cried the boy, while in his joy he hammered with his heels on the soldier's breast. "Ah! here come the altar-boys. How I wish I were with them!" said he, and, the next moment, with a "Thank you, sir," he slid to the sidewalk, and was off toward the cathedral.

7. When the crowd dispersed, the sol-

dier walked about the city, but afterward strolled back to the cathedral to see the procession returning. Imagine his astonish- ment, when among the altar-boys, in red cassock

and white surplice, he spied his young friend.

8. As long as the procession remained in the cathedral, the boy was not noticed, but when he went to the sacristy to disrobe, the priest who was master of ceremonies at once detected the strange face.

"Who are you?" he asked, severely. "How do you happen to have that cassock on?"

9. "Please do not scold me, Father," replied the boy. "A kind soldier let me sit on his shoulders to see the procession, and when I saw a number of boys whom I know marching along, I could not keep from joining them. I know where the cassocks and surplices are kept, so I slid down, ran to the sacristy as fast as I could, and dressed myself. Then I cut across the city, came up with the procession, and here I am."

10. As he stood in the red cassock, his face bright with happiness, the sunlight, creeping through a stained glass window, shed round him a halo of gold. "Do not be angry with me, Father," he continued earnestly. "I was so happy, and it was all so beautiful!"

11. "So you would like to be an altar-boy, eh?" asked the priest.

"O, indeed, indeed I would!"

"Then come with me," said the priest, and the two went out of the sacristy together.

Language Lesson.

Let the answers be in complete sentences.

1. What is the feast of Corpus Christi?
2. What did the boy say to the soldier?
3. Where did the boy seat himself?
4. What was the order of the procession?
5. Where did the soldier next see the boy?
6. What was the result of the conversation between the priest and the boy?
7. What word in paragraph 7 means the same as *scattered?*
8. What word in paragraph 7 means the same as *walked leisurely?*
9. What word in paragraph 8 means the same as *discovered?*

LESSON IX.

knew	wāv'ing	whĭzzĕd	de-şẽrvĕş'
clásp	fĭf'teen	wound'ed	dĭ-rĕe'tion
brĭsk	Chĭ-nĕşĕ'	(woōnd'ed)	hŏs'pi-tal
pẽrchĕd	chăp'lạin	vĭe'to-rў	dĭf'fi-eul-tў

Dictation Exercise.

The bird was *perched* on the branch of a tree. — Father James was appointed *chaplain* of the regiment. — At first I did not know the man, but now I *recall* where I met him. — The stone the boy threw *whizzed* past my ear. — I was *wounded* in the hand by a knife.

One Good Turn Deserves Another.—(*Continued.*)

1. Fifteen years later, a French general lay wounded on a battle-field in

China. The battle was not ended, and it was probable that the soldier would lie on the ground for some time; just then a chaplain passed.

2. "You are wounded, general," said the priest, as he bent over him.

"Yes; I am wounded in the leg. I can not put my foot on the ground."

3. The priest looked steadily at the wounded man, as if trying to recall something, and then said: "Suppose I try to carry you on my shoulders, general. I can take you to the hospital wagon, which is not far off."

4. With some difficulty and much pain, the general got on the chaplain's back, who then set off on a brisk run. Now and then a ball whizzed past them. "That must be meant for me," the chaplain would say. "You have had yours," and he laughed as heartily as a boy.

5. As they neared the hospital wagon, shouts of victory were heard. The Chinese fled in every direction, and the French flag was seen waving in triumph.

6. "Is it not a beautiful sight, general?" cried the priest, as he caught sight of the flying flag. "Almost as beautiful as the one I once saw from your shoulders."

"As you once saw from my shoulders?" said the general. "What do you mean?"

7. "Do you not remember the boy who perched on your shoulders one Corpus Christi? I am he. I knew your face as soon as I saw you, and thank God," he continued with a hearty clasp of the hand, "I am able to serve you now. One good turn deserves another."

Language Lesson.

Let the answers be in complete sentences.

1. Who lay wounded on a battle-field in China?
2. Who spoke to the wounded general?
3. Who was the chaplain?
4. What is a chaplain?
5. Who was the general?
6. What is meant by "a hearty clasp of the hand"?

Let the pupils copy the following sentences, putting quotation marks at the proper places.

That must be meant for me, the chaplain would

LESSON X.

dis-grāçǫ'   sēạ'ṣǫn   tăl'ents

The Sunflower's Lesson.

1. A nice little Sunflower, just over the
    way,
Is blooming four inches tall, I should
    say,
And what is the reason it blossoms
    so low?
Has bright little Sunflower forgotten
    to grow?

2. O, no! but the season is getting
    quite late;
The frosts will be coming, and so it
    can't wait.
It seems to be saying, the Sunflower
    so small,
Better blossom thus low than not
    blossom at all!

3. This lesson I read in the Sunflower's
    face:
To fill well a low place is not a dis-

Make the most of your time, and
your talents tho' small:
Better bloom in low place than not
bloom at all.

Language Lesson.

Of what words are "tho'" and "can't" a short
form? Write the words out in full.

*Let the pupils change the verses into prose, and make the
statements in their own language.*

LESSON XI.

prowl	sĭṇ'glę	ŏb'jeet	aє-єount'
єrạẉl	ŭt'terş	pro-єūrę'	in-єlīnęd'
u-nītę'	brī'dlę	dăṇ'ględ	de-serībę'
zє'brȧş	sĕl'dȯm	єlŭtch'eş	Ăf'rĭ-eạ
ạ-voidş'		un-ū'şu-al	nĕç'es-sa-rў

Dictation Exercise.

Give me an *account* of your travels ; *describe* them
to me. — If you know where I can *procure* an
eagle, tell me, so that I can get it.— The traveler
fell into the *clutches* of the savages, who, as soon
as he was in their power, put him to death.

The Lion.

1. Some writers describe the lion as
brave, and fearless of danger; while
others say he is a coward, and no
more to be feared than a big dog.
Both are right: a hungry lion will face

any danger to procure food, while one that has had plenty to eat will seldom attack man or beast.

2. Like most animals of the cat family, the lion is inclined to take life easy, and will take no more trouble than is necessary to get food. If he can strike down a deer or one of the smaller animals with a blow of his paw, he will not seek more difficult game.

3. The lion does not come out boldly and chase his prey, but creeping toward it from behind a bush or tree, he springs upon it, and strikes it to the ground.

4. The lion's voice is of great help to him. When at night he finds no prey, he puts his mouth close to the earth, and utters a roar which rolls along the ground, and is heard by every animal that is near. Not knowing whence the terrible sound comes, the frightened beasts, wakened from their sleep, run about wildly, often into the clutches of the waiting lion.

5. A number of lions often unite to attack large animals. Many zebras were

quietly feeding on a plain, when several lions, hidden among thick reeds, crept toward them, in single file. Suddenly, the leading lion sprung over the reeds, seized one of

the zebras, and set the others scampering toward his companions.

6. Lions that have never known man are not afraid of him, but when they have learned something of him and his ways only great hunger can make them attack him openly. A lion avoids any unusual object, and will not go near anything that looks as if it were a trap; a white rag waving over

dead game will keep lions from touching it; they have been known to prowl around a lost horse for a whole day, afraid to touch it on account of the bridle that dangled from its neck.

˙ 7. A hunter in Africa, who was returning to his wagon, suddenly came face to face with a lion. The man was out of powder, and had no means of defending himself. Like many people in that country, he wore a large .felt hat, with several feathers on it. Pulling off his hat, and taking it between his teeth by the brim, so that only the upper part of his face could be seen, he dropped on his hands and knees, and began to crawl toward the lion. Such a strange sight was too much for the "king of the forest"; he turned and fled.

Language Lesson.

1. What is meant by the following expressions?
"inclined to take life easy"; "procure food";
"creeps toward his victim"; "utters a roar";
"run into the clutches of the waiting lion";
"in single file"; "dangled from its neck."
2. Who is called the "king of the forest"?
3. Why is he so called?

LESSON XII.

soil	boilęd	rōạst'ed	prŏp'er
eŏbẹ	fôrmęd	kĕrn'elẹ	eăp'tạĭn
māĭzę	blādęẹ	fŭr'rōⱳẹ	är'ti-elęẹ
fū'el	hŭsks	Ęu'rópę	ăl'eo-họl
brọạd	fŏd'der	prŏd'uets	de-lĭ'cioŭs
prĭn'çi-pal		€ō-lŭm'bus	

Maize, or Indian Corn.

1. When Columbus returned to Europe, after the discovery of America, he took with him, among other products of the New World, some maize, or Indian corn. This vegetable, the great captain reported, was one of the principal articles of food in America. It was tried in Europe, and soon grew in favor there.

2. This is not to be wondered at, for no matter how corn is cooked, whether boiled, roasted, or ground into meal, it is one of the most delicious foods that God has given us.

3. The Indians did not raise as good corn as we do to-day, for they were not farmers. Their time for planting it was when the leaves on the white oak

farmers say that the proper time is when
the apple blossoms begin to fall, that is,
about the last of May.

4. Corn needs rich soil and plenty of
hot weather; if the ground be wet and
cold, the seed corn will rot. In preparing land for corn, the farmer plows it
well, and then lays it off in furrows
about three feet apart. At the points
where these furrows meet about five
kernels of corn are dropped; these are
then covered with earth, and, in this
way, little hills are formed.

5. In about two weeks, if the weather
be fine, the young corn begins to appear. At first it shows tiny, tender
blades of green, but its stalks soon
shoot up, and the beautiful broad leaves
unfold.

6. The uses of corn are many. The
ripe grain furnishes food for man and
for horses, pigs, and poultry; besides,
sugar and alcohol are made from it.
The leaves and stalks are excellent
fodder; the dried husks make sweet,
cool beds; and the dried cobs are used
for fuel.

Language Lesson.

1. What is meant by the following expressions?
"other products of the New World"; "the
great captain"; "soon grew in favor there";
"rich soil"; "in furrows"; "kernels of
corn"; "its stalks soon shoot up."
2. To what does the word "this," at the beginning
of paragraph 2, refer?
3. Mention some of the uses of corn.

Add er and est to each of the following words:

broad	deep	fair	tall
sweet	loud	small	young

LESSON XIII.

slĕpt	wā′ģeş	Flŏr′encĕ	po-şĭ′tion
eŏp′ў	eŏl′orş	re-wạrd′	plet′ūrĕş
fĭf′tў	sẽrv′ĭçĕ	lŏdġ′ĕd	chär′eōạl
găr′ret	fămĕd	brŭsh′eş	Tḩŏm′as
shĕl′ter	păl′açĕ	in-strŭet′	€ŏr-tō′nä
	sĭt′ū-ā′tion		re-joi′çing

Dictation Exercise.

A servant, or one who serves, is said to live at
service. —One who has a desirable situation is
said to have *a good position.*

The Cardinal's Lodger.

1. One morning, nearly three hundred years ago, a young boy stood in
front of a cardinal's palace in Florence. Suddenly, a hand was laid on

his shoulder, and a voice exclaimed,
"Why, Thomas, how do you do?"

2. Turning, Thomas found himself
face to face with a boy about his own
age. "What! Peter, is it you?" he cried,
joyfully. "How are all the folks in
Cortona?"

"They are all well," answered Peter,
"but I have left there. I am tired of
tending sheep,—stupid things. I want
to be a painter, and have come here to
learn."

3. "A painter, eh? Have you any
money?" asked Thomas.—"No; none
at all," replied the other. "I am as
poor as a church mouse."—"Then you
might better take a place here, in the
kitchen, where I work. You will, at
least, be sure to have enough to eat."

"No," said Peter, "I do not wish to
enter service; I want to be a painter;
but if you will let me stay with you till
I earn some money, I will pay you
back."

"Agreed," answered Thomas, after a
moment's thought. "Come up to the
garret, where I sleep."

4. So the two boys went to the little room. It was small and very plain ; the only furniture was a straw bed and two old, broken chairs. But it was a shelter, at least, and here Peter settled down.

5. As neither of the boys had any money, Thomas got a piece of charcoal from the kitchen, and with this Peter drew on the wall pictures of men and women, birds and beasts, trees and flowers, till there was no room for more.

6. The day that Thomas received his first wages was a day of great rejoicing in the garret, for now Peter could have paper and pencil, brushes and colors. After that the boy went to work with a will. He drew every thing he could find : the pictures in the churches, the statues in the streets, and even the hills around the city. When night came, he would go back to the room in the garret, where he was sure to find something to eat.

7. No one knew that Thomas had any one staying with him, but the cook often said he ate a great deal for a boy

of his size, and thought it strange he did not grow larger.

8. One day the cardinal happened to enter the garret, where the boys roomed. "Why, whose work is this?" he asked in surprise, when he saw the drawings on the wall. "Who has this room?" When he learned that a poor boy slept there, he sent for Thomas, and said kindly, "You are no longer a kitchen boy, my son."

9. The frightened boy, who thought he was about to lose his situation, fell on his knees, and cried: "Do not send me away. We have nowhere to go, and Peter will not be able to become a painter."

10. "Who is Peter?" asked the cardinal.—"The boy who stays here with me. He drew these pictures that you see; it will break his heart if he can not be a painter. He is out in the streets now, looking for something to draw. He goes out every day, and does not return till night."

"When he comes back to-night, bring him to me." said the cardinal.

11. But Peter did not return that
night. Day after day went by, and
nothing was heard of him. At last, the
cardinal caused a search to be made for
the missing lad, and he was found in a
neighboring convent, where he was making a copy of a picture by a great artist,
and the monks not only allowed this,
but lodged and fed him during the
time he was at work.

12. The cardinal sent Peter to the

best school of painting in Florence, and as a reward for his kindness, Thomas received a good position, and had teachers to instruct him.

13. Fifty years later, two old men lived happily together in a beautiful house in Florence. One was known as Peter of Cortona, and people said of him, "He is the greatest painter of our time;" the other was called Thomas, and was famed for his charity.

Language Lesson.

Fill the blanks in the following statements with the words young, cheerful, stupid, small.

The boy was . . . . . .   He had a . . . . voice.
The sheep are . . . .   The room was . . . . . .

Unite the first two statements by and, omitting unnecessary words.

Familiar Talks on Common Things.

LINEN.—From what is linen made? Linen is made from the threads in the stem of the flax-plant.

Where does this plant grow? Flax grows in Ireland, Holland, Germany, Russia, and the United States.

What do we get from the seeds of the flax-plant? From the seeds of the flax-plant we get linseed oil and meal, and oil-cake, with which cattle are

What is damask? Damask is linen with figures woven in it; so called from Damascus, in Syria, where it was first made.

Which is the finest kind of linen? The finest kind of linen is cambric; so called from Cambray, in France, where it was first made.

WOOL. — From what is woolen cloth made? Woolen cloth is made from the fleece, or hair, of the sheep.

What is worsted? Worsted is the name given to the coarser kinds of woolen stuff. It is also the name of the woolen thread, or yarn, used in knitting stockings.

What is merino? Merino is a fine woolen cloth; so called from the Spanish merino sheep.

Does all merino wool come from Spain? Not all the merino wool comes from Spain: the merino sheep is now reared in Australia, and much of the merino wool comes from there.

What is alpaca? Alpaca is a silky woolen cloth, made from the hair of the alpaca sheep, which lives in Peru, in South America.

Which is the finest kind of woolen cloth? The finest kind of woolen cloth is cashmere, made from the wool of the Cashmere goat.

SILK. — From what is silk made? Silk is made from the fine threads made by a caterpillar called the silk-worm, and wound round its body before it turns into a chrysalis.

Where did the silk-worm first come from? The silk-worm first came from China, whence it was brought by two monks; but it is now reared in all the warmer countries of Europe, especially in France.

What is satin? Satin is a closely-woven and

What is velvet? Velvet is a thick silk, or silk and cotton, cloth, with a shaggy pile on the surface.

What is velveteen? Velveteen is cotton velvet; an imitation of silk velvet, made of cotton.

What is crape? Crape is a kind of gauze, made of raw silk, and stiffened with gum-water.

PAPER. — From what is paper made? Paper is made from linen and cotton rags, from wood, and from different kinds of straw.

From what does paper take its name? Paper takes its name from the *papyrus*, a plant formerly used by the Egyptians for writing on.

How are paste-board and card-board made? Paste-board and card-board are made by pasting and pressing together several layers of paper.

LEADPENCILS. — Of what are leadpencils made? Leadpencils are made of a mineral known as graphite, and sometimes called plumbago, or black-lead.

Copy the names of the months.

January   July
February   August
March   September
April   October
May   November
June   December

LESSON XIV.

fāte	grïef	ăct'ed	brŏŏk
hŭsh	brōōd	€on-tĕnt'	sphēr℮ş
blŭn'der	mŭt'ter℮d	wĭst'ful-lўֿ	

Dictation Exercise.

The little chickens were covered with *downy*, or soft, feathers. — The old duck waded into the water, followed by her *brood,* that is, the ducklings that were hatched at one and the same time.— The child looked *wistfully,* or earnestly, at the cakes. — The man met his *fate,* or death, while out hunting.—We should live contentedly in our *spheres,* or places in society.

The Chicken's Mistake.

1. A little downy chick one day
    Asked leave˘ to go on the water,
  Where she saw a duck with her brood
      at play,
    Swimming and splashing about her.

2. Indeed, she began to peep and cry,
    When her mother would not let her,
  "If the ducks can swim there, why can't
      I?
    Are they any bigger or better?"

3. Then the old hen answered, "Listen to
      me,
    And hush your foolish talking,
  Just look at your feet, and you will see
    They were only made for walking."

4. But chicky wistfully eyed the brook,
    And didn't half believe her,
For she seemed to say, by a knowing
    look,
    Such stories could not deceive her.

5. And as her mother was scratching the
    ground,
    She muttered lower and lower,
"I know I can go there and not be
    drowned,
    And so I think I'll show her."

6. Then she made a plunge where the
    stream was deep,
    And saw too late her blunder;
For she had hardly taken time to peep,
    When her foolish head went under.

7. And now I hope her fate will show
    The child my story reading,
That those who are older sometimes
    know
    What you will do well in heeding;

8. That each content in his place should
    dwell,
    And envy not his brother;
For any part that is acted well

9. For we all have our proper spheres be-
low,
And 't is a truth worth knowing:
You will come to grief if you try to go
Where you never were made for go-
ing.

Language Lesson.

Of what words are "didn't" and "I'll" a short
form? Write the words out in full.

*Change the verse into prose, and make the statements in
your own language.*

LESSON XV.

fĕnçĕ	hōạrsĕ	ôr'di-na-rўˇ
a-lŏft'	nā'tĭvĕ	mĕạṣ'ur-ing
ereeks	nĕ'grŏĕṣ	(mĕzh'yur-ing)
kĭạkĕd	o-pŏs'sum	de-strŭe'tĭvĕ
squeezĕ	eăpt'ûrĕd	es-pĕ'cial-lўˇ

The Opossum.

1. The opossum, by mistake called
the possum, is a native of America. It
is about the size of a large cat, being
rather more than three feet in length,
the head and body measuring about
twenty-two inches, and the tail fifteen.

2. The opossum is a destructive ani-

corn, berries, and almost everything
that comes in its way. Not content
with the food it finds in the open country, it steals into the poultry-yard and
makes a meal of the chickens and their
eggs. As it can climb any ordinary wall
or squeeze through any fence, it is difficult to keep it out of the farm-yard.

3. When the pleasant days of spring
come, the opossum, half starved through
the winter, sets out in search of something to eat. It visits the ponds and
creeks, and snaps up the young frogs
that may be about, or feeds on the tender and juicy stems of the poke-weed.
The call of the wild turkey is like sweet
music to the opossum's ears, for it soon
finds the nest, and feasts on the eggs.

4. Traveling along, perhaps on the
ground, perhaps aloft from tree to tree,
it makes its way toward a farm-yard.
With great care, it creeps along, till at
last it reaches the hen-house, in which
it hides. As soon as the sun has set,
and darkness approaches, the opossum
begins its meal with a dozen or more
eggs, and then seizing the plumpest

chicken, runs off to its home in the woods.

5. If an opossum that has been captured be struck or kicked, the creature rolls over like a ball, and appears to be dead. But it is only "playing possum," for no sooner has its enemy gone than it is on its legs again and off for the woods.

6. If chased by a dog, the opossum takes to a tree, and climbs to some branch just out of reach, where it sits quiet-ly, while the dog barks till he is hoarse.

7. The flesh of the opossum is white, and when cooked is considered excellent food, especially when the animal is fat; negroes are very fond of it. A "possum hunt," which is generally at night, is looked upon as great sport.

8. The opossum, though cunning in many respects, is very simple in others. Hardly any other animal is so easily caught, for it will walk into almost any trap. When captured, it is easily tamed, and soon becomes used to its new home.

Exercise in Articulation.

Pronounce the r in the following words:

cure	hear	our	very
fare	poor	road	your

Copy the names of the days of the week.

Sunday   *Wednesday*
Monday   *Thursday*
Tuesday   *Friday*
       Saturday

LESSON XVI.

pûrsᶒ	Păr'ĭs	pĭt'ĭĕd	dᶂoŭb'lᶒd
ᵉoinɡ	frown	pŭz'zlᶒd	fĭ'nal-lў
frăɳes	tĕᶏᶳᶒd	fä'mᶂŭs	al-low'anᶜᶒ
ᵉon–ᵉlūd'ed		ᶜo-chin' (ko-shăn')	

Dictation Exercise.

Look more cheerful, my child; I do not like to
see a *frown* on your face. The priest was *famous*
for his charity.

Father Cochin's Miracle.

1. When the famous Father James
Cochin was studying to become a priest,
his father allowed him fifty francs a
month for pocket money. The greater
part of this sum the young man gave
away in charity, and the end of the
month usually found him with an
empty purse.

2. One day, as James was out walking, he met a poor woman who told
him that her children had nothing to
eat and her husband was sick and out
of work. The young man listened to
her story, but, though he pitied her, he
had nothing to give. However, the
woman begged him to search his pock-

ets, as it might be that God would work a miracle, and put some money there.

3. To prove that he had nothing, James was about to turn his pockets inside out, when he felt something hard in one of them, and to his great surprise he drew out two gold coins. These he gave to the woman, who, smiling through her tears, exclaimed, "Did I not tell you so! a miracle!"

4. James was greatly puzzled at this. Where had the money come from? He was sure he had none of his own, for he had given his last coin to a poor man some days before. He thought it over, and finally concluded that it was certainly a miracle.

5. In the evening, when he returned to the college, his room-mate met him with a frown, saying, "A pretty trick you played on me! I had to stay indoors all day, because you took my coat, and I could not find yours."

"Your coat!" exclaimed James.

"Yes, my coat; and to prove it, you will find my money in the right-hand pocket."

6. The money was gone, so there was nothing for James to do but to tell the whole story. Of course, his school-mates teased him about it, but his father was so pleased, when he heard of his son's charity, that he not only sent James the two coins to give back to his room-mate, but doubled his monthly allowance.

7. Years after, when James was a priest, he built a hospital for the poor, which you can see to-day, if you go to Paris. He probably never worked any miracles, but he spent his life in helping the poor.

Language Lesson.

Explain the words of similar sound but different meaning.

1. *Some* people spend a great deal of money.
   A hundred dollars is a large *sum* to many folks.

2. Did you *write* the letter, as I told you?
   Be sure to get the *right* address.

3. His coat was made of *coarse* cloth.
   Of *course*, his school-mates teased him.

4. James has a *new* hat.
   I *knew* he would get one.

5. The boy tore the paper in *two ;* it is *too* bad.

LESSON XVII.

eȧst	hẏmn̤	nā'val	fôr'tress̤
Bärt	tow'er	pȧs'tor	ŏf'fi-çerş
stȧid	eär'go	pŭb'lie	bär'gain
wīvȩş	sē'eret	här'bor	Dŭn̤'kirk
Eṉ'glish (ɪṉɡ')		ăp'pe-tītȩs	

How the Tower was Saved.

1. In the winter of 1662, a French
fleet entered the harbor of Dunkirk, a
seaport of France which, at that time,
belonged to England. The news soon
spread, and before long the sailors and
fishermen, followed by their mothers,
wives, and children, hurried to welcome
their countrymen.

2. Then the people of Dunkirk
learned that the king of France had
bought back the town from the English.
This seemed good news indeed, but the
older and wiser men shook their heads
sadly; they talked with their priest,
and did not part till they had agreed
to meet that night in his garden.

3. There was one woman in Dunkirk
who had staid at home, and when Bart,
the fisherman. and his two bovs reached

their cottage, they found it bright and warm, with hot tea and brown cakes awaiting them.

4. "Why, what is the matter?" asked Bart's wife. "Have you lost your appetites in the open air? Dunkirk again belongs to France; this ought to be good news."

5. "So it would be," answered her husband, "were it not part of the bargain that every public building must be cut down till it is no higher than the highest dwelling. No one cares for the fortress — that can go; but to see the old church tower torn down almost breaks my heart. Why, the light from that tower has flashed out on the waters, guiding sailors and fishermen, since my grandfather's time. Who will dare now to cast a net? What vessel will dare come in now for a cargo? Tear down the tower, and Dunkirk is ruined."

6. Never before had the light in the church tower seemed to shine so brightly over the dark sea as it did that night. Within the chapel, the

altar-lamp burned steadily as ever, its crimson light falling on the holy priest, who knelt at the altar praying for his people.

7. Silently, or talking in whispers, the fishermen gathered in the garden. Soon their pastor joined them, and then one plan after another was offered for saving the tower; but none was of use, and the meeting was about to break up, when Bart's younger son, John, asked leave to speak.

8. "Speak, my son," said the priest. "The wisdom of God has often been kept from the great, and made known to the little ones."

9. "Father," answered John, "since no public building may be higher than the highest dwelling, there is only one way to save the tower; let a dwelling be made of the same height. Tear down our cottage to-morrow night, and before morning breaks build it as high as the top of the church tower; thus will the tower, the city, and the fisheries of Dunkirk be saved."

10. It was all the priest could do to

keep the men quiet. "My children,"
said he, "you see how the good God
protects you. As for you, my son,"
laying his hand on the head of the
happy boy, "you will become famous,
and your mother will be proud of you."

11. The following night the French
commander gave a ball on board of his
ship, to which he invited the English
officers, and while they enjoyed themselves, the common soldiers made merry
on shore.

12. In the meantime, the people were

was carried to the priest's garden, where the women kept watch, while the men were hard at work.

13. Within the chapel, the good priest prayed; now and then, as the sound of the hammers reached his ear, he asked a blessing on the strange work, but, more than all, he returned thanks to our Lord, who had whispered to a child the secret by which Dunkirk would be saved.

14. When morning broke, the rough fishermen joined in the hymn of praise sung by the priest of God, and the breeze bore their voices over the water. Standing on the decks of their vessels, the French and the English officers saw a fisherman's cottage reaching high in the air, even above the church tower. From its roof waved the flag of France, while through the open door could be seen Bart, the fisherman, with his wife and boys, joyful that the tower was saved.

15. John Bart, in time, became a brave and famous officer, proving the truth of the good priest's words.

Language Lesson.

What is meant by the following expressions:
" A French *fleet* entered the harbor." "The news
soon spread." " No one cares for the *fortress.*"
"The light from that tower has flashed out
on the waters, guiding sailors and fishermen,"
etc. "To *cast* a net." "Come in now for a
cargo." "The meeting was about to *break up.*"
"When morning *broke.*"

LESSON XVIII.

skĭll	chĭps	a-wạrd'	măj'es-tў
queer	deeḍṣ	eăl'i-eo	de-elârĕd'
chĕạt	be-g̃ăn'	blŭshĕd	op-prĕsṣĕd'
swĕpt	wor'thў	wĭn'ner	ad-mĭt'ted
	re-grĕt'ted		stăm'merĕd

Dictation Exercise.

To whom did the teacher *award*, or give, the prize
for "good conduct"? I read the other day of
an unjust king who so *oppressed* his people that
they rebelled, and drove him from his country.
A king is addressed as "Your *majesty,*" on account of his high rank.

The Prize Winner.

1. A king once ordered a trial of good
deeds among his people, and offered to
give the winner whatever he might select as a prize. There had often been

trials of skill; but in the first, the strong oppressed the weak, in the second, the swift did not help the slow, and in the third, one tried to cheat the other. This, therefore, was the first trial with a really good object.

2. A day was set for this new trial, and the following morning the people were to meet at the palace, where, one by one, they were to be admitted to tell the king what good they had done.

3. When the time came, many were the queer stories told. One man said he had searched through the kingdom, but could not find any good deed to do.

"Hem!" said the king, "you might, at least, have mended your clothes. That would have been better than nothing."

4. Another allowed that he had seen many *little* things to do, but had hurried on all day in search of some *great* thing worthy of a prize.

"How foolish!" cried the king; "do you not know that you can reach the great only by way of the little?"

5. A third declared he had given in charity half of all he owned.

"And if I award you the prize, what would you choose?" asked the king.

"May it please your majesty," quickly answered the man, "I would like to have one of your palaces."

"Any one of which, as you well know, is worth a hundred times all you have given," said the king. "The prize is not yours."

6. And so it went on, till at last the king regretted he had offered a prize, for he began to understand that good deeds are often done only for the sake of a reward.

7. Last of all came a little girl; she had on a plain, clean, calico dress, her hair was neatly brushed, and her blue eyes had such an honest look, that the king felt sure she had done better than any of the others. But she had come only to look on, and when the king asked what good deeds she had done, the child answered, "May it please your majesty, I had no time yesterday to do good deeds."

8. "No time for good deeds!" said the king; "pray, what were you doing?"

"Mother was busy," replied the child, "so I fed the chickens, picked up chips, swept the kitchen, set the table, and played with baby to keep him still."

9. "Good," said the king, "but did you not want to try for the prize?"

"O, yes, indeed," answered the little one, "because there is something I want very much; but I had to give it up, for I was too busy. I do not know how to do good deeds, anyhow."

10. "I think you do," said the king, "and I intend to give you the prize. So now, my child, tell me what you would like."

The little one was surprised; she blushed and stammered, and it was only because she desired the prize so much that, at last, she answered, in a voice hardly louder than a whisper, "May it please your majesty, I would like a little wagon for baby to ride in." She received not only what she wished for, but much more.

Language Lesson.

Let the pupils fill the blanks in the following statements.

1. A king ordered a trial of . . . .
2. The king offered to give the winner a . . . . . .
3. The little girl's hair was neatly . . . .
4. The little girl had only come to . . . .

Exercise in Articulation.

Pronounce the wh in the following words :

where	white	wharf	whisper
which	whence	whether	whistle

LESSON XIX.

ä-hä'	pạusẹd	hånd'sȯmẹ
Ꮯhrīst	ĕr'rand	mĕn'tionẹd
Sā'tan	fârẹ'wĕll	wor'shippẹd
ġī'ant	trĕm'bling	wạn'der-ing
mär'tўr	Ŏf-fĕr'ro	ꞓon-vĕrt'ing
hĕr'mit	de-vout'lў	Ꮯhrĭs'to-pher

The Legend of St. Christopher.

1. There was once a mighty giant, named Offero, who was famous for his great strength and size. So proud was he of these gifts, that he started out to find the most powerful prince in the world, determined to serve him alone. At last, he entered the service

of a king whom he believed to be the greatest one on earth.

2. All went well, till one day the name of Satan was mentioned, when the king devoutly crossed himself.

"Why do you do that?" asked the giant.

"To protect me from the Evil One, whom I fear," answered the king.

"You are afraid of him!" exclaimed Offero; "then he must be greater than you. Farewell. I go to seek him, that I may serve him."

3. Leaving the good king, Offero started off to find Satan. As he was about to enter a thick wood, he was hailed by a handsome man, standing by the roadside.

4. "Who are you?" asked Offero.

"I am Satan," answered the stranger. "I was waiting, for I knew you would come this way. Enter my service, and I will give you pleasure and wealth."

"I do not care for them," said Offero; "what I want is to serve the greatest of all kings. When I find him, I will be his slave."

"Then come with me," replied Satan, "for I am the greatest; all fear me."

5. They started off together, but had not gone far when they passed a wooden cross, at sight of which Satan paused.

"Why do you stop?" asked Offero.

Satan grew pale. "Come, let us hurry away," he cried; "I can not bear the sight of that cross."

"Why, you are trembling!" said the giant.

"Yes, yes; I fear Christ," whispered the Evil One.

"Aha! then you are *not* the greatest king of all," shouted Offero. "Farewell. I go to seek your master."

6. One day, as the giant was wandering about, asking where he could find Christ, he met a pious hermit, to whom he told his errand. Bidding the giant sit down, the good man related the story of our Lord's life.

7. Offero's heart warmed with love for this new master, but he feared he could be of little use to Him. "I have nothing but my great strength to offer," he said, "and of what use is that?"

Then the hermit led him to a river,
which ran so swiftly that hundreds
were drowned in it every year, and

bade him live beside it, and help people who were trying to cross. This
Offero did, and saved many from the
angry waters.

8. One night, the giant found a child standing by the river side waiting to cross. Placing the little one upon his shoulders, Offero began to wade across the stream. But the weight of the child, which was as nothing at first, became so great that the giant cried out, "Who art Thou, O Child! Had I the whole world upon my shoulders, it could not be heavier."

"Wonder not, O Christopher," replied the Child, "for thou hast upon thy shoulders not alone the world, but Him who made the world."

9. Then the giant's eyes were opened, and when he reached the shore, he knelt, and worshipped the Savior of the world. From that day, Offero was known as "Christopher," which means "Christ-bearer." Nor did he ever forsake this best of masters, but preached His word, converting many, and finally had the happiness of dying a martyr for Him who died for all.

Language Lesson.

Omit the last letter in each of these words, and add ing:

take   give   serve   come   make   have

LESSON XX.

tŏnᶒ	Sä′rȧ	rĭd′dᶒn	mŏd′est
dĭnᶒ	twĕlvᶒ	eom′erṣ	seôrn′fṵl

shăb′bi-lȳ   ae-quäint′ançᶒ

ex-eläim̦ᶒd′   fäsh′ion-a-blȳ

Dictation Exercise.

Ned is a proud boy, and speaks in a *scornful,* that is proud and overbearing, way to poor people.— The old gentleman always has his coat made in a *special* way, that is, in a way different from others.

A Daughter to be Proud of.

1. When Mr. Lent visited New York last summer, he called at the office of his friend West. After a long talk about old friends and old times, they parted, but not until West had made his friend promise to dine with him the following day. "For," said he, "I want you to make the acquaintance of my wife and daughter."

"Have you only one child?" asked Mr. Lent.

"Only one," answered West, "but she is a darling."

2. Among the many sights of New York, Mr. Lent wanted to see the beau-

tiful Central Park; so, on leaving his friend, he stepped into a horse car.

3. In a short time, four girls, each about fifteen, entered the car; they were fashionably dressed, and each carried a lunch basket. Mr. Lent learned, as they laughed and talked, that they, too, were on the way to the Park.

4. They had not ridden far when the car stopped to take on a girl of twelve and a sick boy of four. The new-comers were shabbily dressed, and as they seated themselves at the lower end of the car, they looked anything but happy.

5. "I suppose *they* are going to the Park," said one of the four girls, with a nod towards the poor children.

"I suppose so," answered one of her companions, in a scornful tone, "but I would rather stay at home than go in such shabby clothes."

"Yes, indeed," said another. "I think there ought to be special cars for the lower classes."

6. This was not spoken in a loud voice, but Mr. Lent knew that the poor

felt angry, and was about to tell the
young ̇ "ladies" what he thought of
them, when one exclaimed, "Why, there
is Sara! I wonder where she is going?"

7. Mr. Lent turned to look; at the
same moment the car stopped, and a
modest young girl came in.

Language Lesson.

What is meant by the following expressions:
"make the acquaintance of"; "a delicate girl";
"a special car."

LESSON XXI.

hŏst	bọ̈-quet'	ĕx-ăet'lȳ
flŭsh	(bōō-kā')	fôrt'ū-natẹ
smĕlỉ	ad-drĕss̩'	nōtẹ'-bŏok
ẉrōtẹ	grăt'i-fȳ	ĭn'-tro-dūç'ing

Dictation Exercise.

The *host*, or owner of the house, met me at the
door. — I knew the present would *gratify*, or
please, the child, and when she saw it first a
flush, or sudden flow of blood, spread over her
cheeks. — Afterward, she *related*, or told, the
story to her mother.

A Daughter to be Proud of.—(*Continued*).

1. The new-comer was warmly wel-
comed by the four, who made room for
her beside them. "Where are you go-

flowers!" said another, as she bent over to smell them. "For what fortunate one are they intended?"

"I am going to Jane Hall's," said Sara in answer to both questions. "She is sick, and I thought these flowers might gratify her."

2. Just then Sara noticed the poor children. Crossing over, she gently laid one hand on the little boy's head, and asked, "What is the matter with this little fellow? He does not look well."

3. Sara's smile was so pleasant, her manner so gentle, that the poor child felt she was a friend. "We do not know exactly," she said; "Danny has never been well. I am taking him now to the Park, to see if the air will make him feel better."

4. "I am sure it will," said Sara. "It is lovely there; everything smells so sweet and pure. But you ought to have brought your lunch along, for the air will make you hungry."

5. A flush passed over the little girl's face. "Yes, we ought to, but, you see, we had none to bring. Our brother

Tom, who works, saved these cents so that we could ride to the Park and back. May be Danny will forget to be hungry, there will be so much to see."

6. There were tears in Sara's eyes as she listened; she inquired where the children lived and wrote the address in a little note-book.

7. After riding a short distance, Sara left the car, but where she had found two sad children, she left two happy ones. Half of her bouquet was in the little girl's hands, while Danny held a well-filled lunch basket, from which he helped himself now and then.

"She said we could eat it all," he whispered delightedly to his sister — "every bit of it. What made her so good to us?" The little girl whispered in answer: "Because she has a good heart."

8. When the Park was reached, the four girls hurried out. Mr. Lent carried Danny out of the car and into the Park, and before leaving slipped some money into the little girl's hand. "That is for a ride in a Park carriage," he said.

9. The following day he called at Mr. West's house. "This is my wife," said the host, introducing a pleasant-looking lady, "and this," as a young girl entered the room, "is my daughter."

10. "Ah!" exclaimed Mr. Lent, as he took the girl's hand, "this is the dear child whom I saw yesterday in the street car. She is, indeed, a darling. God bless her," and then he related to his friend what he had seen and heard.

Language Lesson.

Write six statements, using one pair of the following words in each sentence:

I	ate	bad	by	bear	be
eye	eight	bade	buy	bare	bee

LESSON XXII.

fïerçę	a-mūş'eş	strŭg'glę
tī'ger	tıī'flıng	ex'hi-bĭ'tion
eon-veẍ'	en-gāġęd'	re-ar-rān'ġeş
erŭsh'ing	ĕl'e-phant	dis-săt'is-fıęd
im-pōşęd'	ex-ăm'ınęd	im-mē'di-atę-lў

The Elephant.

1. The elephant as we see it on exhibition is very different from the animal

amuses by a few trifling tricks; there, it does a great deal of useful work. It plays the part of the laborer and porter, piling up wood and carrying coal, loading and unloading boats, and lifting heavy weights. It also takes the place of the nursery maid, carrying children about in safety, and gently rocking them to sleep with its great trunk.

2. The elephant has been taught to act the part of a stone-mason, and build a wall. It places the stones in position, steps back to see that they are properly laid, and then, if dissatisfied, returns, and re-arranges them.

3. A story is told of an elephant that was thus engaged in building a wall. Every time a row of stones was laid, the animal made a sign for the overseer to look at the work. If all was right, the elephant continued its task. After a while, it grew tired and careless, but that it might not be obliged to do the work over, it placed itself close to the wall, so that the job could not be properly examined.

posed on, however, and ordered the beast to stand aside. When the cunning creature found its trick was discovered, it immediately began to tear

down the imperfect wall, and from that time did its work properly.

5. A few years ago, in India, pipes had to be laid to convey water over hills and through woods where there were no roads. The distance was nearly

two miles, and elephants were employed to assist in the undertaking.

6. It was interesting to watch the animals at work. Lifting a heavy pipe, and balancing it on its trunk, an elephant would march off with the load, and carry it safely to the place where it was to be laid. Once there, the beast would kneel, and place the pipe just where the overseer wished it. At one time, when an elephant found that a piece of pipe would not fit into another, the beast put its head against the end of the pipe, and forced it into place.

7. The wild elephant appears to be feared by most of the other animals. When a herd of elephants approaches a stream to drink, the other beasts, with scarcely an exception, retire and stay away till the giants have slaked their thirst.

8. Although usually gentle, the elephant at times becomes excited, and will then attack anything that comes in its way. Even the fierce tiger, of which the elephant seems naturally

afraid, then finds his match. A fearful struggle follows the meeting of these two powerful beasts. Round and round they circle, each watching its chance, till, with a sudden bound, the tiger springs upward, and fastens his teeth and claws on the giant's shoulder or back. Mad with pain, the elephant wraps its trunk round the body of its foe, tears the tiger from his place, beats him against the ground, and generally ends by kneeling on him, and crushing out his life by the weight of its great legs and heavy body.

Language Lesson.

The name given to a person in baptism is called the *Christian* name.

A person's last name is his *family* name, or *surname*.

Give examples of Christian names and of family names.

LESSON XXIII.

plăn	frŏl′ĭe	pēr′sǫn	buṣ′i-lȳ
blīthę	lēącnęd	hĭn′derṣ	(bĭz′i-lȳ)

The Boy who Helps his Mother.

1. As I went down the street to-day,
　　I saw a little lad
　Whose face was just the kind of face
　　To make a person glad.

It was so plump and rosy-cheeked,
    So cheerful and so bright,
It made me think of apple-time,
    And filled me with delight.

2. I saw him busily at work,
    While blithe as blackbird's song
His merry, mellow whistle rung
    The pleasant street along.
"O, that's the kind of lad I like!"
    I thought as I passed by;
"These busy, cheery, whistling boys
    Make grand men by-and-by."

3. Just then a playmate came along,
    And leaned across the gate—
A plan that promised lots of fun
    And frolic to relate.
"The boys are waiting for us now,
    So hurry up!" he cried;
My little whistler shook his head
    And "Can't come," he replied.

4. "Can't come? Why not I'd like to
        know?
    What hinders?" asked the other.
"Why, don't you see?" came the reply,
    "I'm busy helping mother.
She's lots to do, and so I like
    To help her all I can;
So I've no time for fun just now,"
    Said this dear little man.

5. "I like to hear you talk like that,"
   I told the little lad;
   "Help mother all you can and make
      Her kind heart light and glad."
   It does me good to think of him
   And know that there are others
   Who, like this manly little boy,
   .Take hold and help their mothers.

Language Lesson.

1. Of what words are the following short forms?
   "I'd"; "don't"; "I'm"; "she's"; "I've."
2. What word in the second line of the second
   stanza means the same as *joyous?*

LESSON XXIV.

Dūkę	bûr′dęn	pŏv′er-tȳ
eōṳrt	per-mĭt′	re-stōręd′
fōrçęd	de-elīnę′	ae-çĕpt′ed
gṳĕsts	weep′ing	Hŭṇ′ga-rȳ
thrōnę	ex-trēmę′	mĭs′er-a-blę
älmş′gĭv-ing		mŏn′as-tĕr′ȳ

Dictation Exercise.

The king received a number of *guests,* or visitors
whom he entertained, at his court. —My aunt
has an *income* of two thousand dollars a year,
much of which is spent in *almsgiving*.

St. Elizabeth.

1. This great Saint was a princess of
Hungary, but instead of giving herself

up to the pleasures of the court, she spent her days helping the poor. She built several hospitals, where she served the sick with her own hands.

2. Once, as she was going through a forest, carrying in the folds of her cloak food for the poor, she met her husband, Louis, who was returning from the hunt. Seeing his wife bending under the weight of her burden, Louis opened the cloak, which she held closely wrapped around herself, and, wonderful to tell, found in it nothing but beautiful roses, although it was not the season for flowers.

3. Louis knew that it was a miracle; he bade his wife continue on her way, but took one of the roses, which he kept during his life.

4. Some time after, Louis went to the war, where he was killed. In spite of the loving charity of Elizabeth, her husband's brother, the Duke Henry, cruelly turned the holy princess and her little children out of the palace. It was mid-winter, and the cold was very

she had helped in many ways, the un-
grateful people refused her shelter, for

they feared the anger of the Duke,
should they assist her.

5. The weeping woman and her little
ones went from door to door, but no-

where was she admitted, not even to the houses of those who, at one time, pretended to be greatly attached to her.

6. At last the princess came to an inn, and as this was a house open to all, she refused to be turned away. The inn-keeper gave her, as a resting place, a miserable out-house. It was a poor shelter, but there the wanderer remained till midnight. Then, when the bells of a neighboring monastery began to ring, Elizabeth rose, and, taking her children, went to the church, where she thanked God for the troubles with which He had visited her.

7. The Saint passed the rest of the night and part of the next day in the church, until the extreme cold and the hunger of the children forced her out again to beg for food and lodging.

8. In vain she went through the town, till at last a priest, very poor himself, took the homeless wanderers into his humble dwelling. Elizabeth gratefully accepted his kindness; the priest prepared a room for his guests, and cared for them as well as his poverty

would allow. After a time, Elizabeth and her children found a home in a convent.

9. When the soldiers who had been with her husband returned from the war, they offered to place the princess again on the throne, but this she declined, and was content with having her rightful income restored. Elizabeth passed the rest of her life in prayers and almsgiving.

Language Lesson.

1. Explain the meaning of:
   " she built several hospitals "; " it was not the season for flowers "; " they feared the anger of the Duke "; " her rightful income."
2. What other words could be used instead of "spent her days"?
3. When does winter begin?
4. When is mid-winter?
5. Mention some of the troubles with which God visited St. Elizabeth.

Exercise in Articulation.

Pronounce c hard in the following words:

ache	became	crown	uncle
active	courage	direct	excuse

Pronounce ç soft in the following:

ice	cell	palace	necessary
face	grace	conceal	excellent
twice	fancy	receive	innocence

LESSON XXV.

hĕạp	făn'çў	bĕn'e-fĭt
shârẹ	tăst'ed	de-spīşẹd'
ḳnŏbş	snĭffẹd	spĕç'i-men
in-sĭst'	făm'ĭnẹ	ae-eôrd'ing
mã̱ẋ'or	Īrẹ'lạnd	eŭl'ti-văt-ed

Dictation Exercise.

I do not like that dress; I do not *fancy* the color. — A number of people died during the *famine,* that is, during the time that food was scarce. — She put the flowers to her nose and *sniffed* at them. — That is a fine *specimen* of penmanship.

The Potato.

1. The potato, like maize, is a native of this country. These two vegetables are America's gift to the world, and of all her gifts they are the most valuable.

2. The potato was taken to England in 1623, but, at that time, received very little attention. Nearly a hundred years later, people thought it might be used as food for swine and cattle, and might, perhaps, even prove of use for the poor. Finally, the potato was cultivated and grown in Ireland, and from there was carried to England, where, in a short time, it came into general use.

3. In Germany, the new vegetable did not find favor with the people, and the government had to insist upon its use. There had been a terrible famine in parts of that country, and the following year large wagon-loads of potatoes were sent to the market-places of the different towns.

4. Meetings of the people were called, and every owner of garden land was told to go to the town-hall, at a certain time, as the king intended to give each a present. When the people reached the hall, the mayor showed them the new vegetable, which, till then, they had never set eyes on, and read plain directions for planting, tending, and cooking it.

5. The people took the highly praised brown knobs in their hands, smelled them, licked them, tasted them, and then, with a shake of the head, passed them to their neighbors. Some broke off pieces, and threw them to the dogs; they sniffed at them, but left them untouched. "Ha!" said one man, "these things have no taste and no smell, and

even the dogs will not eat them; how can they benefit us?"

6. However, the king's commands were obeyed, and each land or garden owner received a measure of potatoes. Very few understood the directions that had been given for the care of this vegetable, so some threw away their share, while others set to work to plant it according to their fancy. The potatoes were stuck here and there in the ground, and no more trouble was taken with them. In other cases, they were put together in a heap, and covered lightly with earth.

7. When the king learned that some of the people despised his gift, and had not even taken the trouble to plant it, a potato show was held, and any one who did not send a specimen of the potatoes he had grown was fined. This only made the potato disliked more than ever. The next year, the king again sent some potatoes to each town, and with these sent men who showed the people how to plant them. In time, every one learned to like the potato.

and now there is no vegetable more generally used.

Add ly to each of the following words. Afterward, write eight statements, each containing one of the newly formed words:

brisk	loud	quick	stiff
firm	modest	proud	quiet

LESSON XXVI.

thĭrd	Gus-tävệ'	ęom-pŏg'er
fŏg'gў	vī'o-lĭn'	fa-mĭl'iar
mĭn'glệ	show'erệd	per-fôrm'erş
yọ̤ths	ap-plạụsệ'	çĕl'e-brāt-ed
ap-plạụd'ed		ęon-sŭmp'tion

Dictation Exercise.

Charles is *familiar,* that is, well acquainted, with the English language.—The king *showered,* that is, bestowed liberally, his favors on the man.

A Noble Three.

1. One foggy night in winter, many years ago, a feeble old man stood in the streets of a large city, trying to draw music from a ·violin. But his fingers were too weak or too cold, and no one stopped to listen to him. Sad and weary, he sat down on the sidewalk, laid his violin across his knees, and

said, "God help me! I can no longer play!"

2. At that moment, three young men, laughing and singing, came down the street. They did not see the old violinist, and as they hurried along, one struck against him, the second fell over him, and the third stepped back in surprise as he saw the man rise from the ground.

3. "I beg your pardon," said the first, as he picked up the man's hat, "I fear we have hurt you." Then seeing the violin, he continued, "Are you a musician, sir?"

"I used to be," answered the poor man, as two big tears rolled down his cheeks, "but I can play no more. My fingers are stiff with age. What shall I do! What shall I do! My daughter is dying of consumption and of want."

4. The young men were moved with pity, but, alas! they had no money. "Friends," said Charles, "this will never do. We must help this man; he is a brother musician. Here," he said to one, "you play his violin while Gustave

sings, and I will take up the collection."

5. Taking their places, they began. The playing and singing were both fine,

and soon drew a crowd which applauded and showered money on the performers, while the old violinist beat time. Song followed song, each gaining more

had all he could do to gather up the coins that fell round them.

6. When the music stopped, the crowd broke up. "Noble youths," said the old man, "let me know your names that my daughter and I may mingle them with our prayers."

"My name," said the first, "is Faith."

"And mine," added the second, "is Hope."

"While mine," said the third, as he poured into the old man's hat the money that had been collected, "is Charity."

7. "Ah, gentlemen!" said the grateful old man, "how can I thank you? With this money I can return to the village in which I was born, where my daughter will be cared for. Her native air may restore her health. As for you, God will reward you for your charity, and you shall become great among the great."

"Amen," answered the young men, cheerfully, as they joined arms and walked away.

one of the young men became a violinist of great fame, another, a singer cel-
ebrated throughout the world, and the
third a composer whose name is familiar wherever music is known.*

Language Lesson.

Words like *Gustave, Adolphe,* and *Charles,* are called
proper names, or *proper nouns.* A proper name
always begins with *a capital letter.* Words like
man, violin, ground, musician, are called *common
names,* or *common nouns.*

LESSON XXVII.

firm	en-a'blẹ	vȧ'ri-ȯŭs
gnạ̄ws	eon-sĭsts'	çĭr'eu-lar
grōōvẹ	trămp'ling	păs'saġ-eṣ
re-ṣĭst'	eon-strŭet'	eon-nĕet'ed

Dictation Exercise.

The boy made the snow as hard and *firm* as a rock
by *trampling,* or treading, on it.—The old dog is
hungry; see how he *gnaws* the bone.—If you are
tempted to do wrong, fight against the tempta-
tion; *resist* it.—I hired a carpenter to *construct,*
or build, my house.

The Beaver.

1. The beaver is a water-loving animal; he never walks when he can swim.
He has close, woolly fur, a broad, flat

* The name of the singer was Gustave Roger; the violinist,
Adolphe Hermann; the collector, Charles Gounod.

tail, and is web-footed, that is, his toes are connected by a thin skin, to enable him to swim easily.

2. During the summer, the beaver lives by himself in a burrow, but as winter comes on, two or three hundred of these animals sometimes unite to build a town. They begin by selecting a place, generally on the bank of a river. The next step for the beaver, is to construct a dam across the stream near which he lives, so that it may not run dry. As wood is needed for this, a point is chosen where the river is narrow and is overhung by trees.

3. The beaver is not only a builder, and a wonderful one at that, but he is also an excellent wood-cutter. Having selected a tree, he cuts it down, using no tools but his own sharp teeth. Sitting upright, he gnaws a hollow groove, or cut, round the trunk of the tree, till little of the wood is left, then he gives two or three powerful bites,

and the tree falls to the ground. Afterward, the animal cuts the trunk into pieces about a yard long.

4. To make a dam, logs are laid across the river, and covered with stones and earth till they can resist the force of the water. All the time they are at work, the beavers move to and fro, trampling down the soft earth with their paws, and making it smooth. When logs are needed, the beavers float them down the river, but stones and earth are carried between their forepaws and lower jaw.

5. Great numbers of logs are thus placed, and mud and stones are added from time to time till the dam becomes as firm as the land itself. Some dams are very large, being two or three hundred yards in length, and ten or twelve feet in thickness.

6. When the dam is finished, the beavers begin to build their town. The houses are made of mud and branches, in the same way as the dam. They are all built close to the water, and passages lead from them into the ground in va-

rious directions. The door of the house is under the water, generally three or four feet below the surface.

7. The shape of the houses is nearly circular. Each house has two rooms, one above the other, and is large enough to hold several beavers; they live in the upper room, the lower one being used to store food, which consists, principally, of bark.

8. Like the bird and the bee, the beaver builds his house just as God has taught him, and it never changes. The beaver's house is the same to-day as it was a hundred years ago.

Exercises in Articulation.

Drill the pupils in pronouncing ing in the following words:

barking	coming	giving	entering
bedding	calling	dashing	dancing

LESSON XXVIII.

pĭtch	brĭdġĕ	brṳiṣĕd	stā′tion
hāstĕ	frẹiġht	un-lĕsṣ′	wạrn′ing
	ex̱-ẽr′tions̱		pĕr′il-ᴏŭs

Brave Kate.

1. One stormy night in the summer of 1881, the heavy rain swelled a little

creek till the water rose and washed
away the railroad bridge that crossed
it. At the time, no one knew of the
accident, and a freight train that came
along soon after ran crashing into the
creek.

2. A girl of fifteen, named Kate, lived
close to the bridge; hearing the noise
of the falling train, she hurried to the
spot, and, by great exertions, succeeded
in saving the engineer and fireman, who
had gone down with the locomotive.

3. This was a brave deed, but Kate's
work did not stop here. She knew that
a passenger train would pass that way
within an hour, and unless warning
were sent in time, it would fall through
the broken bridge, and hundreds of
lives would be lost.

4. The night was pitch dark, and
the rain was beating down heavily.
The nearest station was almost a mile
distant, and to reach it a long railroad
bridge had to be crossed.

5. It was not easy to cross this
bridge even in broad daylight, and on

But the brave girl did not fear danger to herself, her only thought was to save others; so she started in all haste for the station.

6. Just as she reached the bridge, the wind blew out her light; but even that did not stop her. Getting on her hands and knees, she crawled along the rails, moving carefully from tie to tie, till she had gone the whole length of the bridge; then she rose, and ran as fast as she could.

7. She was bruised and wet, and her clothes were in tatters, as she stumbled into the station. "Stop the train! stop the train!" was all she could say, and then she fainted. But Kate felt well repaid for what she had done; she was in time, and the train was saved.

Language Lesson.

Add ful to each of the following words, and give the meaning of the newly formed words:

| care | joy | fear | pain |
| faith | harm | cheer | peace |

A noun may mean *one*, as, friend, girl. When a noun means one only, it is in the *singular* form.

When a noun means *more than one*, as, friends, girls, it is the *plural* form.

LESSON XXIX.

hūgᵻ	mā′plᵻ	vī′o-lĕt
sĭr′up	drĭv′ᵻn	mo-lȧs′sеṣ
drāinṣ	crŭshᵻd	diṣ-ṣŏlvᵻd′
poundṣ	re-fīnᵻd′	im-pū′ri-tĭeṣ

Sugar.

1. "The rose is red, the violet's blue,
   Sugar is sweet, and so are you."

Thus sung Louise to her little baby-sister. "I do not know whether it is brown sugar or lump, but you are as sweet as both."

2. "It seems to me you are talking a great deal about sugar," said her mother, who was busy sewing. "Do you know where it comes from?"

"Why, I never thought of that," answered Louise, "I suppose it is found in mines, like salt, is it not?"

3. "No, my child. Most of the sugar we use is made from the sugar-cane, which looks much like corn stalks. The cane is from one to two inches thick, and grows to a height of eight feet, and, sometimes, even to twelve or twenty feet.

4. "When the cane is fully ripe, it is

cut a little above the ground, and tied in bundles to be sent to the mill. There it is crushed between huge iron rollers, which press out the juice. From sixty-five to seventy pounds of juice are often obtained from a hundred

pounds of cane.

5. "This juice, which looks very much like dirty water, is boiled till the water is driven out, and nothing but the sugar remains.

"In this state it is known as raw sugar; it is afterward refined, and, in that way, we get the lighter colored

NEW THIRD READER.   111

and white sugars. The sirup which drains from the sugar is called molasses."

6. "How is sugar refined?" asked Louise.—"That I can hardly explain so as to make it clear to you," answered her mother, "but it is dissolved in hot water, and run through charcoal, which cleans it of all impurities."

7. "Is maple sugar made from sugar-cane?"

"No; that is the juice of the maple tree. In the spring of the year, when the juice or sap rises from the roots, holes are bored in the trunk of the tree. The sap which runs out, is caught in pails and pans, and boiled in much the same way as the sugar-cane juice.

8. "In France, Germany, and some other countries of Europe, where there is no sugar-cane, the great part of the sugar is made from the beet-root."

Language Lesson.

Copy and supply words to express kind or quality.

Sugar is . . . . . .
Sugar-cane looks like corn . . . .
Maple sugar is made from the juice of the . . . . .

LESSON XXX.

erāzẹd	mĕr′ri-est	sŏr′rōw-ing
grĭevẹd	Çhär′lottẹ	lạwn′-tĕn′nis
pre-pârẹ′	Rĭv′er-dālẹ	hănd′ker-chĭẹf

A Letter from Agnes.

Riverdale, N. Y.,
July 18, 189–

Dear Sara,

You will be surprised and grieved to hear of the death of our dear friend Charlotte May. It was so sudden that I can hardly believe she is gone from us, and, now and then, I find myself thinking of her as if she were still alive.

Last Friday, we had a game of lawn-tennis on the grounds near our house, and Charlotte was one of the merriest of the party. The day was hot, but in spite of the heat, we enjoyed the game. The time passed so quickly that it was five o'clock before we knew it, and Charlotte had to hurry off, as she had promised to be home in time to prepare supper. Poor dear! how happy she seemed as she ran down the road, waving good-by to us with her handkerchief! We little thought it was good-by forever.

So that she might not be late, she ran almost the whole way home, and reached there greatly overheated. Then, being thirsty, she went into the cellar, and drank some ice-cold milk.

Soon after, Charlotte became ill, and as she grew worse Father Francis and the doctor were sent for. The priest gave her the last sacraments, but the doctor could *not help her, and before midnight our friend was dead.*

Her parents were almost crazed with grief, and have not yet recovered from the shock.

Charlotte was a dear, good girl, and every one loved her; but that is no wonder, for she never spoke ill of any one. Pray for her, Sara, and write as soon as possible to

Your sorrowing friend,

Agnes.

Exercises In Articulation.

Pay particular attention to the accented syllables and the vowel sounds in the following words, which are frequently mispronounced:

wĕrę	dŏç'ĭlę	sĕrv'ĭlę
tū'tor	cléạn'lў	ĭs'o-lātę
a-gain'	eŏl'umḥ	in-quī'rў
(a-ğĕn')	said (sĕd)	mu-ṣē'um
mĭn'ute	new (nū)	il-lŭs'tratę
(mĭn'it)	wạṣ (wŏz)	op-pō'nent
prŏç'esṣ	ĭ'ron (ĭ'urn)	ăd'mi-ra-blę

LESSON XXXI.

sçĕnt	râft'erş	Prĕş'ençĕ
quĕst	ôr'phan	gär'land-ed
ûrġĕd	zĕȧl'ǫŭs	pŏr'rin-ġerş
quȧint	a-māzĕd'	be-wĭl'derĕd

Dictation Exercise.

A *boss,* or large knob, of wood hung from the *raft-ers,* or roof timbers, of the hall. — The men started in *quest,* or search, of the lost boy. — The oatmeal was served in *porringers,* or por-ridge-cups. — The girl was confused, or *bewil-dered,* by the crowd. — The room was *garlanded,* or hung with garlands of flowers.

In the Orphan Home.

1. They sat at supper on Christmas Eve,
     The boys of the orphan-school,
   And the least of them all rose up to say
   The quaint old grace in the old-time
       way,
     Which always had been the rule:
   "Lord Jesus Christ, be Thou our guest,
   And share the bread which Thou hast
       blessed."

2. The smallest scholar sat himself down,
     And the spoons began to clink
   In the pewter porringers one by one,
   But one little fellow had scarce begun
   When he stopped and said, "I think"—

And then he paused with a reddened
    cheek,
But the kindly master bade him
    "Speak!"

3. "Why does the Lord Christ never
    come?"
    Asked the child in a soft, shy way; ·
"Time after time we have prayed that
    He
Would make one of our company,
    Just as we did to-day;
But He never has come for all our
    prayer.
Do you think He would, if I set Him a
    chair?"

4. "Perhaps. Who knoweth?" the master
    said,
    And he made the sign of the cross;
While the zealous little one gladly sped,
And drew a chair to the table's head,
    'Neath a great ivy boss,
Then turned to the door, as in sure quest
Of the entrance of the Holy Guest.

5. Even as he waited, the latch was raised,
    The door swung wide, and lo!
A pale little beggar-boy stood there,
With shoeless feet and flying hair
    All powdered white with snow.

"I have no food, I have no bed;
For Christ's sake take me in," he said.

6. The startled scholars were silent all,
   The master dumbly gazed;
The shivering
   beggar
   he stood
   still,-

The snowflakes melting at their will,—
   Bewildered and amazed
   At the strange hush; and nothing
      stirred,
   And no one uttered a welcome word,—

7. Till, glad and joyful, the same dear child
   Upraised his voice and said,—
   "The Lord has heard us now, I know;
   He could not come Himself, and so

He sent this boy instead,
His chair to fill, His place to take,
For us to welcome for His sake."

8. Then, quick and zealous, every one
    Sprung from the table up.
The chair for Jesus ready set
Received the beggar cold and wet;
    Each pressed his plate and cup.
"Take mine! take mine!" they urged
    and prayed;
The beggar thanked them, half dismayed.

9. And as he feasted, and quite forgot
    His woe in the new content,
The ivy and holly garlanded
Round the old rafters overhead
    Breathed forth a rich, strange scent;
And it seemed as if in the green-hung
    hall
Stood a Presence unseen, which blessed
    them all.

10. O lovely legend of olden time,
    Be thou as true to-day!
The Lord Christ stands by every door,
Veiled in the person of His poor,
    And all our hearts can pray,—
"Lord Jesus Christ, be Thou our guest,
And share the bread which Thou hast
    blessed."

Language Lesson.
Tell the story of the poem in your own words.

LESSON XXXII.

prĭṣ′ǫn	Är′thur	păn′ṣȋeṣ
văl′leẙ	hụr-räḳ′	sue-çeed′ed
thrīvĕṣ	drōōp′ing	ex-çītĕ′ment
stātĕ′lẙ	sŭn′bĕạmṣ	dis-trĭb′ut-ed

Our Lady's Flower Society.

1. From the time that Margaret was a baby, she had been so weak that she had to sit all day in a chair, which her brothers would roll from one window to another, following the sun-beams as they moved.

2. The little girl loved the sun, and always felt better when sitting in it. Her favorite seat was near a window full of flowers. These were her pets, and to each she had given a name. One tall, strong rosebush was St. Christopher; the lilies of the valley, modest and drooping, were St. Agnes; while the stately white lilies were St. Joseph.

3. The spring that Margaret was twelve years old, it seemed as if the weather would never become warm. It was nearly May, but the nights were yet frosty and the days chilly. The flowers

looked as if they wanted to get out in the fresh air, but it was too cold for them.

4. One day, a neighbor who called on Margaret's mother said, as she was leaving, that she and some friends were getting up a flower society, and they would be glad to receive any assistance.

5. "What is a flower society?" asked Margaret, when the neighbor had gone. Her mother told her that it was a society for the purpose of furnishing flowers for the altar, the sick, and the poor. Margaret was very quiet the rest of the day, and when her brothers came in from school, running and shouting, in their rough, boyish way, she told them of the flower society, and said, "We are only children, but I think we might get up one of our own."

6. "Hurrah for Margaret's flower society!" shouted Arthur, as he knocked over a pot of ivy in his excitement.

"That is not to be its name," said Margaret with a smile. "We will call it 'Our Lady's Flower Society,' and we will ask her to make the flowers blos-

som." So "Our Lady's Flower Society"
it was named.

7. At first, Margaret thought to keep
it within her own family, but when the
neighbors' children heard of it, they
begged to join the society, and Margaret was too kind-hearted to refuse
them. She was made directress, and the
others were to do the work. Margaret's
father gave the children a little piece of
ground for a garden, and others presented seeds and plants, hoes, rakes,
spades, and watering-pots.

8. The boys and girls set to work
with a will, and the garden succeeded
famously. When the weather was fine,
Margaret was wheeled out, and then sat
by the hour watching the plants.

9. At last, the long-looked-for day
came when the flowers were to be distributed. The first bouquets were sent
to Our Lady's Altar, great masses of
pansies and lilies of the valley to the
hospital, and even the sick people in
prison were remembered.

10. "I believe you would have cried
with joy, Margaret," said one of the

boys, "to see the sick folks brighten up when Sister let us lay a bunch of flowers on each pillow. We gave a blind man some roses because they smell so sweet, and he said they made him think of heaven. To a poor sick girl we gave bright flowers, and she told us they did her more good than the doctor's medicine."

11. All the long, hot summer, the children kept up their work, and not a week passed without something happening that more than paid them for their labor. Just as autumn was setting in, and the leaves on the trees were turning to brown and gold, a great wonder happened: Margaret got well! or nearly so, for she could walk alone, though slowly. The doctor said it was the fresh air, and having something to think of, but Margaret shook her head. She knew better. She believed that Our Lady had heard the prayers she offered up while sitting among the flowers, "Health of the sick, pray for me!"

12. All this happened six years ago.

The society still thrives, and Margaret, now well and strong, is still its directress.

Language Lesson.

1. What word in paragraph 2 means the same as *hanging down?*
2. What word in paragraph 2 means *tall, high,* or *lofty?*
3. What word in paragraph 4 means *help?*
4. What word in paragraph 7 means *gave?*
5. What word in paragraph 9 means *dealt out?*
6. What word in paragraph 12 means *prospers?*

LESSON XXXIII.

tēạm	trāiled	bŭf'fa-lō
slŭnk	lĭz'ardş	pe-eūl'iar
mōōsẹ	dōōmẹd	thrĕạt'ẹned
găl'lop	whĭppẹd	sŭb'stanç-eş
swŭng	pur-sūẹd'	ae-eŭs'tomẹd

Dictation Exercise.

I do not know the *substances,* or materials, of which this stuff is made, but am sure there is no silk or linen in it.—I stood on a *cliff,* or high, steep rock, looking out to sea.—The lady's dress *trailed,* or dragged, along the ground.—James kicked the dog, and it *slunk* away, or sneaked off.

The Wolf.

1. This dangerous animal is found in almost every part of the world. It is at home in every climate, on mount-

ain and plain, in forest and field. It seems to find enough to eat where another beast would starve.

2. When hungry, which it generally is, the wolf is an animal to be feared; it will run great risks to reach its prey, and will not hesitate to attack even such large, powerful animals as the buffalo, the moose, or the wild horse.

3. The wolf is not particular about its food; it will eat almost anything, from human beings to frogs, lizards, and insects. It will eat even its own kind, and a weak, sick, or wounded wolf is almost sure to fall under the cruel teeth of its companions.

4. Wolves generally hunt in packs, and any animal unfortunate enough to be chased by them is doomed. No matter how swift it may be, the tireless gallop of the wolves will surely overtake it, and no matter how strong it may be, it must at last fall under the repeated and constant snaps of their teeth.

5. There is something peculiar about the bite of a wolf. Instead of biting then holding on, it snaps sharply

fiercely, and so strong are its teeth, that it can bite through substances on which other teeth would not leave a mark.

6. The wolf sometimes shows great cunning in securing its prey. Once, a moose was feeding on a cliff, when a pack of wolves approached. Forming a line, they crept slowly toward the moose, driving it nearer and nearer to the edge of the cliff, till at last, to escape the white fangs that threatened it, the frightened creature threw itself into the valley below. The wolves took a safer path down, and soon

were feasting on the body of the dead moose.

7. Bold as the wolf is when free, it loses all its courage when once within a trap, and will even allow the hunter to drag it out without resistance. It shows great fear of any object to which it is not accustomed, being afraid of even a piece of rope trailed from a wagon or sled.

8. It is related that a man, living in a country place, while driving in his sled was pursued by a pack of wolves. As he was only about two miles from home, he whipped up his horses, and reached the entrance of his house with his pursuers close behind him. The gate was closed, but the frightened team dashed it open and raced in, followed by seven wolves.

9. Just as these savage creatures entered, the gate, fortunately, swung shut, and the wolves were prisoners. When they found themselves shut in, their manner changed, and so far from attempting to attack the man, they slunk away, tried to hide in corners.

and allowed themselves to be killed
without attempting to resist.

Language Lesson.

The *plural* form regularly ends in *s,* or, in certain
words, in *es.*

Write the following words in the plural by adding s:

angel	bead	case	desk
apple	bank	cake	duck

Write the following words in the plural by adding es:

ax	dish	branch	cargo
box	cross	church	potato

Familiar Talks on Common Things.

GLASS. — Of what is glass made? Glass is made
chiefly of sand or flint and potash or soda, melted
together in clay vessels.

What are the principal kinds of glass? The principal kinds of glass are flint-glass, crown-glass, and
plate-glass.

For what is flint-glass used? Flint-glass is used
for making tumblers, wine-glasses, and other articles for domestic use.

How are these articles made into the required
form? Articles of glass are made into the required
form by blowing through a long tube, and by
moulding.

For what is crown-glass used? Crown-glass is
used chiefly for windows.

How is crown-glass made into sheets? Crown-
glass is made into sheets by twirling rapidly a mass
of the soft hot glass on the end of a rod before a
furnace.

What is plate-glass? Plate-glass is the finest kind of sheet-glass, and is made by pouring the melted glass upon an iron table. The surface is then ground and polished.

What is done to all glass after it is made, in order to render it less brittle? In order to render it less brittle, all glass is *annealed*, or slowly cooled, after being brought to a great heat.

SOAP.—Of what is soap made? Soap is made of fat or oil boiled with soda that has been mixed with lime.

What is white soap? White soap is soap made with pure white tallow.

Of what is yellow soap made? Yellow soap is made of resin, and palm-oil instead of tallow.

Of what is soft soap made? Soft soap is made of oil and tallow, mixed with pearl-ash instead of soda.

GLUE. — How is glue made? Glue is made by boiling the parings of hides, and the sinews and hoofs of animals, till they turn into a firm jelly, which hardens as it cools.

How is glue prepared for use? Glue is prepared for use by placing a pan containing the hard glue and a little water in a second pan containing water only. As the water in the latter becomes hot the glue melts.

What is gelatine? Gelatine is a fine kind of glue, prepared from the skins of animals, and used for making sweet jellies.

What is isinglass? Isinglass is a still purer kind of glue, used for the same purposes as gelatine, and made from the sounds, or air-bladders, of certain fishes.

Memory Gem.

LESSON XXXIV.

çĕllş	glōwĕd	for-sāk'ing
strew	dĭ-vīnĕ'	swạd'dling
gŏs'pel	tôrch'eş	Bĕth'lĕ-hĕm
glō'ri-à	quĭt'ted	ō'ver-flōw'ing

The Crib.

1. How beautiful and touching is the sight of a Christmas Crib! What holy and tender feelings fill our hearts as we look on the helpless, little Infant Savior lying in His Blessed Mother's lap, with dear St. Joseph and the shepherds standing by, the patient animals in their stalls, and the Gloria Angel watching over all!

2. It was a loving heart that first thought of making a Crib. It was the heart of a Saint,—St. Francis of Assisi. This Saint was the son of a rich merchant, but for love of the poor Savior he chose to become poor. Whenever Christmas came, his heart glowed with a burning love for the Holy Child Jesus.

3. Once he was sitting at table while the Gospel of Christmas was being read,

and when it came to the part where we are told that the Blessed Mother of God wrapped the Infant Jesus in swaddling clothes, and "laid Him in a manger," Francis rose from the table, and with his heart overflowing with sorrow seated himself upon the ground, saying: "While He who made the world teaches us poverty in the manger, shall I, a sinful servant, sit at table?"

Francis remained seated on the ground, and contented himself with the coarse food eaten by the poor.

4. The Saint often wished he were a rich and mighty king, "for then," said he, "I could have the blessed Christmas kept in every place as a true and holy feast. I would order my servants to strew corn about the streets, so that even the little birds would praise God on that day." He could not do this, so he did what he could to make others love the Divine Infant.

5. He went out to a wood where he prepared a stable in a cave; he

and brought in an ox and an ass.
Over the manger he set up an altar,
so that holy mass might be said there.
When Christmas Eve came, Francis and
the other brothers of his Order quitted
their cells, and taking lighted torches
went to the wood. A crowd of people followed them, singing Christmas
hymns.

6. Then holy mass was said. Francis
served it and sung the gospel; afterward, he preached on the birth of "the
poor King," and spoke with such love
and piety that all were moved to tears.
He called our Savior "the Child," or
"the Babe of Bethlehem," and as often
as he spoke the Holy Name, it seemed
as though honey dropped from his
lips.

7. The place where this first crib was
built belonged to a nobleman. He was
present when Francis preached, and as
he watched the preacher, he seemed to
see the Infant Jesus in the arms of the
Saint. The man's heart was so touched
with love for the Divine Child that he

world, entered the Order of St. Francis,
passing the rest of his life in prayer
and work.

Language Lesson.

Define the words of similar sound but different meaning.

cells   The . . . . . of the prison are damp.
sells   The baker . . . . . his bread.
find   Did you buy that ring or . . . . it?
fined   The man was . . . . . for walking on the
grass.
ob'jects The room was filled with . . . . of art.
objects' James . . . . to leaving home.

LESSON XXXV.

bäth	chĭrp'ing	pāvĕ'ment
răt'tlĕ	mĭs'chĭĕf	flŭt'ter-ing
trŭĕks	sŏ'cia-blĕ	quạn'ti-tĭĕṣ
erŭmḅṣ	(sō'sha-bl)	ĭm'pu-dent-lў

The Sparrow.

1. This bold little bird is as much at
home in the midst of a crowded city as
in the open fields of the country. It
fears neither the heavy farm horse, as
he drags his weary load over the rough
road, nor the noise of carriages and
trucks, as they roll over the city pave-
ment; nor even the roar and rattle of
the cars.

2. Insects and grain are the usual food of the sparrow, but there is scarcely anything that man eats on which it will not feed: it may be seen sharing crumbs of dry bread or bits of potato with its family, and even picking at a bone.

3. In public parks and other places where there are collections of birds and other animals, the sparrow is always found in great numbers, impudently pecking at the food of the caged birds. It will venture even through the bars of the eagle's cage, help itself to the scraps of meat left by the royal bird, and within a yard of his terrible beak and claws splash merrily into his bath.

4. The large animals, too, receive constant visits from the sparrow, which hops about their feet without the least fear, and picks up the scattered grain

5. In the country, the sparrow devours great quantities of grain; but it more than makes up for the mischief it does in this way, by killing many insects. It is a sociable bird, and likes company. It is amusing to watch a flock of the impudent little creatures, fluttering, chirping, pecking, scolding, and fighting.

6. The nest of the sparrow is made of hay, straw, leaves, and twigs, and is always lined with feathers, for though it cares little for frost and snow, it likes a warm bed. The nest is generally built in some sheltered place, such as a hole in an old wall, against the pipes at the sides of houses, or in the gutter under the roof.

7. The voice of the sparrow is a chirp, yet people in the city, who hear no other birds, find it pleasant to listen to a flock of sparrows as they hop about the street.

Language Lesson.

An *action-word*, or verb, is a word that expresses action or being, as, the horse *runs;* the bird *sings.*

LESSON XXXVI.

gāzĕd	wrĕçk	trī'fling
shroud	rāḡ'ing	pïērç'ing
ghȧst'lў̆		shŭd'derĕd

The Little Light.

1. The light shone dim in the headland,
   For the storm was raging high;
I shaded my eyes from the inner glare,
   And gazed on the west, gray sky.
It was dark and lowering; on the sea
   The waves were booming loud,
And the snow and the piercing winter
      sleet
   Wove over all a shroud.

2. "God pity the men on the sea to-night!"
   I said to my little ones,
And we shuddered as we heard afar
   The sound of minute-guns.
My husband came in, in his fishing coat
   (It was wet and cold that night),
And said, "There'll be lots of ships go
      down
   On the headland rocks to-night."

3. "Let the lamp burn all night, mother,"
   Cried little Mary then;
"'Tis but a little light, but still
   It may save drowning men."

"O nonsense!" said her father (he
  Was tired and cross that night),
"The headland lighthouse is enough."
  So he put out the light.

4. That night, on the rocks below us,
    A noble ship went down,
  But one was saved from the ghastly
      wreck,
    The rest were left to drown.
  "We steered by a little light," he said,
    "Till we saw it sink from view:
  If they had only left that light all night
    My mates might have been here too!"

5. Then little Mary sobbed aloud;
    Her father blushed for shame;
  "'Twas our light that you saw," he said,
    "And I'm the one to blame."
  'Twas a little light—how small a thing!
    And trifling was its cost,
  Yet for want of it a ship went down,
    And a hundred souls were lost.

Language Lesson.

Tell the story of the poem in your own words.

What two words does *there'll* stand for?

Memory Gems.

Be slow to promise, but quick to perform.
A young man idle is an old man needy.
Better to slip with the foot than with the tongue.

LESSON XXXVII.

haul	rā'vẹnş	flăn'nelş
chief	răi'şinş	prŏd'ūçẹ
seärf	fäil'ūrẹ	lōnẹ'sòmẹ
grō'çer-iẹş		mĭnçẹ'pĭẹş

Jack's Wood Pile.

1. "Mother, I think I shall haul the wood down to the village to-morrow."

"Very well, my dear," answered his mother. "I shall have some chickens ready for you to take along."

2. Since the death of his father, Jack had been the chief support of his mother and his two little brothers. They lived at least four miles from the village, and not a neighbor was within a mile of them, and were it not for the whistle of the locomotive, as the trains passed through the cut below their house, the place would have been lonesome indeed.

3. Jack was very proud of his wood pile. It had cost him many weeks of hard work, for he had cut and sawed every stick of it himself, and upon it

and clothing for the little family. "I have a cord more than mother thinks there is," he whispered to his brothers, "and with the money I get for that I mean to buy all sorts of nice things— apples and raisins—and may be mother will make us some mince-pies for Christmas."

4. The next day, Jack started with the first load of wood, his head full of plans for extra comforts for his mother and brothers. When he drew up in front of the little store in which the country folks traded their corn, wheat, and other produce for groceries and dry-goods, the owner was standing at the door.

5. "No, I do not want any wood," he said in answer to Jack's question. "I bought a piece of woodland last summer, and I have cut my own wood this year, and supplied every one around here.— No, I do not want any chickens, either; but if you are very anxious to trade, I will take what you have at three cents a pound."

6. No wood wanted! Poor Jack could hardly keep back the tears; the

scarf for his mother, the mittens for the boys, flannels, and other necessaries were all gone in a minute. Three cents a pound for chickens! It would pay better to eat them than to sell them at that price. However, he parted with a few to get some things his mother could not well do without, and then turned his mules homeward.

7. Jack did not unload the wood when he reached home, but left it standing. Snow had been falling for some time, and as the boy walked toward the house, after putting his mules in the stable, the ground was quite white. In a few words, Jack told his mother of his failure to sell the wood, and then seated himself by the fire, resting his head on his hands.

8. "I do not know what we are going to do," he said after a while, in a tone that spoke more than his words.

"Nor I, Jack," said his mother, putting her arm tenderly round him; "but, my dear, we are not expected to know. It is only our Lord who knows. We must wait and trust."

9. "I wonder how things would go on if we would just sit down and trust."

"But we do not sit down and trust. We do our best, and when we have done that, all we can do is to trust. Those were almost the last words your dear father said to me. He saw what was coming, but he felt that God, who feeds the young ravens, would not forget us. Have faith and hope, Jack, my boy, have faith and hope."

Language Lesson.

Explain the words of similar sound but different meaning.

The air of the room is *foul.*
The *fowl* are in the barn-yard.

My *dear* child, respect old age.
A young *deer* is a pretty animal.

We must all *die.*
Wash the *dye* off your hands.

LESSON XXXVIII

| nōtĕs | frīĕd | fĭg′ūrĕ | bŭs′tlĕd |
| gŭĕsš | squârĕ | bush′elš | a-mounts′ |

Jack's Wood Pile—(*Continued*).

1. The snow fell thick and fast through the night, and the following morning Jack could hardly make his

way to the stable to feed the cow and
the mules.   When he did succeed in
getting there, he met a sight that surprised him.   In the railroad cut stood
a long train of cars half-buried in the
snow.   A number of men were trying
to clear a path before the engine, while
others were passing Jack's load of wood
into the cars.

2. "Halloo!" cried a man who was
directing the workmen, "do you know
whose wood this is?"

"It is mine," replied Jack.

"Well, if you have any more, I want
it, — all you have.   Can you bring it
here?"

"As soon as I can dig it out of the
snow."

"My brakemen will help you," said
the man, who was the conductor of
the train.   "We are in a bad fix.   We
have been here all night, and are likely
to be here all day.   My passengers
must not freeze.   Bring all the wood
you can."

3. Jack hurried to give his mules

eating, he ran to tell his mother the good news.

"Did I not tell you to have faith and hope?" said his mother. "Our dear Lord never forgets those who trust in Him."

4. Jack worked like a hero that morning, and when he carried the first armful of wood into a car, what a shout of welcome he received from the half-frozen passengers!

5. "See here," said the conductor, when the fires were well started, "do you know where we can get something to eat?"

"We have plenty of chickens and potatoes and corn-meal, and my mother can cook them," answered Jack.

"And we will help, if she will let us," said three ladies.

6. Jack's mother and the lady passengers were soon at work, and before long steaming, mealy potatoes, hot corn-bread, and delicious fried chickens were served to the grateful passengers.

7. About noon, the conductor bustled

said, "and I want to square accounts
with you. We pay three dollars and
a half a cord for wood. Just see what
that amounts to. Then there are three

o r
four dozen chick-
ens, bushels of
potatoes, and the best
corn-bread I ever tasted. I
am in too great a hurry to figure
it all out, but I guess this will pay for
it," laying some bank-notes on the table. "If that is not right, just send to
the address on this card. Good-by!
Thank you," and before Jack's mother
could say a word the man hurried

8. When Jack ran down to see the train off, he was received with cheers.

"Here," said a man, picking up a train-boy's basket, "let us give them some books and papers; they are always welcome in the country."

"Yes, and so are other things," said a lady who had noticed the poverty of the house; "here is a shawl for Jack's mother."

9. That started it, and as the basket passed from one car to another, mittens, caps, scarfs, and overshoes were thrown in. Those who had nothing else to spare tied a little money in their handkerchiefs, and threw them in, and, last of all, one man gave an overcoat for Jack. Then the basket was lifted off the train, and put at the boy's feet, and with the passengers crying, "A merry Christmas, Jack!" and, "Three cheers for Jack's mother!" the train went on its way.

Language Lesson.

What is meant by the following expressions: "A railroad *cut*"; "in a bad *fix*"; "worked like a hero"; "square accounts"; "*address* on this

LESSON XXXIX.

eälm	dĭ-vīd'ed	in-creäsĕd'
mĭdst	Ăn'ge-lŭs	af-flĭe'tions
vīrt'ûę	re-lĭg'ĭọŭs	eom-plāinĕd'
mär'riĕd	mûr'murĕd	sur-round'ed

St. Germaine Cousin.

1. In the year 1579, a girl was born in a village of France who was baptized Germaine. A sickness, from which she never recovered, troubled her from her birth, and, besides, her right hand became useless. To add to her afflictions, her pious mother died. Some time after, her father married again, and then Germaine's troubles began in earnest.

2. Her stepmother treated her with great unkindness. In spite of the child's feeble health, the cruel woman sent her into the fields, often in stormy weather, to tend sheep. Her food was coarse bread, her dwelling a sheep-cot, with straw for her bed.

3. Germaine never complained, but was always calm and cheerful. Her day's duties were simple. She rose at

and then drove them to the pasture. When the bell rang for the Angelus, she knelt to pray, wherever she might be, sometimes on the stony ground, sometimes on the damp earth.

4. She went to Mass every day, no matter how bad the weather was. In the pasture fields she fixed on a tree a rude cross, made of two strips of wood, and before this she knelt and prayed. When not praying, she was thinking of God, and this filled her heart with love and joy.

5. One winter night, some villagers, passing near the girl's sheep-cot, heard the sound of music. They drew near, and, looking through a crack in the door, saw Germaine kneeling in the midst of her sheep. Her hands were raised toward heaven, a halo of light shone around her head, and the sound of heavenly music filled the air.

6. Germaine could never see any one in want or sorrow without wishing to help him. Although her only food was a piece of dry bread, she divided that among those poorer than herself. Once,

she went without food for a whole week, that she might give the bread to a sick person. The poor children of the village, who loved her for her gentleness, gathered around her in the field where she watched, and listened to the lessons of piety she taught.

7. Thus did Germaine live; seldom free from pain herself, she was always trying to help others. She never murmured, but patiently doing the will of God, waited for Him to call her to Himself.

8. One morning, as she did not lead her flock to the pasture, as usual, her father went to call her. She made no reply; he entered, and found her lying dead on the rough bed. She had fallen asleep in prayer, and her soul had flown to heaven.

9. On the day of Germaine's death, two religious, who were on their way to the village, were obliged to remain over night in the forest. Suddenly, the woods became brighter than at midday, and the astonished religious saw a number of young girls dressed

in white, each surrounded by a halo of light, moving toward a poor cottage, which they entered. In a few minutes, they re-appeared with one more added to their number.

10. The religious were filled with joy at this sight, for they knew a holy soul had gone to heaven. As soon as it was day, they hurried to the village, and described their vision. Then they learned that a young girl had died during the night, and when asked to point out the house seen in their vision, they immediately selected the cottage in which Germaine had lived.

11. The neighbors, who for a long time had considered Germaine a saint, came in crowds to look upon her, and to ask her prayers. The fame of her virtue had spread far and wide, and increased after her death; she was buried with every mark of love and respect.

12. Forty-three years later, a man, while digging a grave, found the body of a young girl who appeared to be asleep, so natural and lifelike did she look. It proved to be the body of Ger-

maine, which our Lord had preserved
as a mark of His love for this faithful
servant.

Language Lesson.

Explain the words of similar sound but different meaning.

The color of the sky is *blue*.
The wind *blew* hard.

The young lady is well *bred*.
Your mother makes excellent *bread*.

Fred bought two pencils for a *cent*.
The *scent* of the rose is sweet.
Luke was *sent* on an errand.

The day is warm and *fair*.
How much is the *fare* to Boston?

James sold the baker twenty barrels of *flour*.
Which is your favorite *flower*?

LESSON XL.

thĭrst	ĭn'ju-rў	re-quīrĕs'
eăm'el	ob-jĕets'	grōăn'ing
thôrnṣ	stŏm'aeh	wĕïgh'ing
elŭm'ṣў	growl'ing	gär'ments

The Camel.

1. The camel is a homely-looking
animal. He is large and clumsy: has a
small head, a long neck, long, slender
legs, and a great hump on his back.

2. But despite his looks, the camel is

loads a great distance over sandy deserts under a broiling sun. His toes are broad and his feet are made so that he can walk with ease on the smooth, slippery sand. As the camel has to kneel often, while being loaded, there are thick, hard lumps upon his knees and breast which support his weight when he is kneeling, and save the skin from injury.

3. In crossing a desert, it is often impossible to procure water for several days, but the camel drinks large quantities of it before starting on a journey, and is then able to go nearly a week without a further supply. For food he eats almost everything: even the hard, dry thorns that are found here and there in the desert, which no other creature would touch.

4. The camel can easily carry a load weighing five or six hundred pounds, but he objects to carrying any load at all; his keeper has to force him to kneel, and, when down, he ties his neck and fore-legs together. While this

continual growling and groaning, and bites at any one who comes near; from this it is easy to see that his temper is as ugly as his looks.

5. The deserts are great plains of sand on which, for miles, not a drop of water nor a blade of grass can be

found. Some of these deserts are very large. It requires more than three months to cross the Great Desert in Africa. Here and there are green spots and wells of water, at which travellers stop to rest and refresh themselves and their beasts.

6. It sometimes happens that no water can be had and the travellers

are dying of thirst. In such cases, a camel is killed, and the suffering men save themselves by drinking the water found in the camel's stomach.

7. The hair of the camel is of much value. In his own country, it is spun into strong thread of which tents and coarse rugs and carpets are made; with us, it is used for making paint brushes. The fine wool found on some parts of the camel's body is spun and woven into garments; shawls made from it bring extremely high prices.

Language Lesson.

Let the answers be in complete sentences.

The camel's appearance.—Is the camel a handsome animal?

The value of a camel. — Where is the camel most valued?

Why is the camel valued?

The hair of the camel.—For what is the camel's hair used?

The food of the camel.—Of what does the camel's food consist?

The camel's temper.—Has the camel a good temper?

A desert.—What is a desert?

Life on a desert.—What are travellers on a desert sometimes obliged to do?

Memory Gem.

It is never too late to learn.

LESSON XLI.

doubt	stärt'lĕd	un-gāin'lў̃
êrⱕ (âr)	quạr'terṣ	slŭm'berĕd
Ăr'abṣ	per-çĕïvⱕ'	suf-fī'cient

The Camel's Nose.

1. The Arabs tell of a miller
Who one morning, from his repose,
Was awakened by hearing a camel
Through the window thrust his nose.

2. "It's cold out here," said the creature,
"And I wish, sir, if you please,
Just to warm my nose a moment;
It's so chilled I fear 'twill freeze."

3. "All right," said the other kindly;
"You do look pinched and thin."
"O, thank you!" replied the camel,
And his head came further in.

4. Soon, while the miller slumbered,
Both head and neck were through;
Then, presently, in at the window
The body entered, too.

5. Now, the room was close and narrow,
And the startled sleeper woke,
And to his ungainly inmate
At length complaining spoke.

6. "Really, my friend, while willing
     To grant your first request,
   My quarters are not sufficient
     To hold so large a guest."

7. "Very well," said the other, coolly,
     "If you find it as you say,
   Move out—in fact, you'll have to,
     For I have come to stay."

8. How plainly this story teaches
     (As you perceive, no doubt)
   Wrong into the heart admitted
     Will soon the right drive out.

9. And how plain it warns us, also,
     At the very first to shun
   The evil that seems so harmless,
     Ere an entrance has been won.

Language Lesson.

Of what words are *'twill, you'll* short forms?
Write the words in full.

What words could be used instead of the following, and convey the same meanings? "Repose,"
"chilled," "slumbered," "presently," "startled,"
"ungainly," "inmate," "request," "quarters,"
"perceive," "warns," "ere."

Tell the story of the poem in your own words.

Commit to memory the last eight lines of the poem.

LESSON XLII.

Neïl	hătch'et	ar-rängĕd'
pshaw	bī'çy-elĕ	blăɛk'smith
fōụrth	Lĕọn'ard	fīrɛ'erăɛk'erş
at-tĕnd'	va-ea'tion	săt'is-făe'tion

Faithful in Little Things.

1. "There is no use talking about it any more. I have to ride Bay Billy round the pasture till he is tired, and then go down to the post-office. So I can not go with you and the other boys, much as I would like to go."

2. "Pshaw, Neil! What is the use of working all the time? I think a boy ought to have a vacation once in a while."

3. "I can do what I like in the afternoon," answered Neil, "but father thinks a boy ought to learn to do all sorts of work, and he knows."

4. "May be," said Leonard, as he turned to leave. Then looking back he called out: "Did I tell you, that my father is going to buy me a bicycle next week?"

5. "No," replied Neil. "You are in luck. I wish I could have one."

When Neil put the letters in his father's hands, on his return from the post-office, he saw among them a bicycle circular. "How I wish I could have a bicycle, father," he said.

6. "Well, my boy, I am willing you should have one," answered his father, "when you earn it." .

Neil's face fell at this, for he saw little chance of being able to earn enough money to buy anything so costly. "Leonard's father has promised to buy one for him," he added.

7. His father looked up. "He has, eh? Well, let me know the size of it when he gets it, will you? Has Leonard any work to do for his father?"

8. "No; he keeps out of the way till his father leaves in the morning, and is always asleep when he returns at night."

9. "Keeps out of the way, does he?" said Dr. Fox. "Well, my boy, if, at any time, you should see something you think ought to be done, I hope I can

rely upon you to do it, without being told."

"I think you can, father," replied Neil.

10. "Very well," said the doctor. "By doing your duty in little things you may, in time, gain large rewards. At any rate, you have the satisfaction of knowing you have done what you ought to do." As the doctor was leaving the room, he added, "Do not forget to let me know when Leonard gets his bicycle."

11. The next day was the third of July, and Dr. Fox was to leave home to attend a meeting of doctors to be held in the city. He expected to return on the afternoon of the Fourth, and the day following he intended to drive Bay Billy to a horse fair.

12. The doctor left no tasks for Neil, so he and a party of boys arranged to go berry picking on the Fourth, and as they had plenty of firecrackers, they expected to have great fun.

13. The morning of the Fourth was lovely, and, after breakfast, Neil started

out to meet his comrades. As he was going by the pasture, he stopped to speak to the horse, and as he did so, the beast held up a hoof from which ·the shoe was dangling.

14. "O, dear!" said Neil, "why did you show me that now? I can not help you, old fellow." The hired men had all gone off for a holiday, and there was no one but Neil to take the horse to the blacksmith, who was three miles away. The boy knew that it would take most of the day to have the horse shod, as there were always so many horses waiting, and that meant giving up his day's pleasure.

15. It was a hard trial, but while Neil was thinking about it, Leonard came up. "Come along, Neil," he said, "the boys are waiting for you." That settled it. Neil remembered what his father had said about doing what he thought ought to be done, and his mind was made up. "I am not going," he answered. "I have to take the horse to be shod," and he walked away.

16. The hatchet needed grinding, so

he went to the house for it, and then returning, mounted the horse, and rode slowly to the blacksmith's, taking care that Bay Billy should not get lame from fast driving.

Language Lesson.

A *quality-word*, or adjective, is a word that expresses the kind or quality of the thing named, as, a *handsome* bicycle; an *obedient* boy.

Let the pupils copy the following, and supply the quality-words:

"By doing your duty in . . . . . . things."
"The morning of the Fourth was . . . ."
"It was a . . . . trial."

LESSON XLIII.

chĕck	ĕx'trȧ	de-prīve'
rēạrĕd	trȧinṣ	tŭg'ging
brākĕs	e-vĕnts'	drŭnk'ẹn
	cóm-pârẹd'	swĭtch'man

Faithful in Little Things—(*Continued*).

1. When Neil reached the blacksmith's, it seemed as if every horse for miles around was waiting to be shod. But Neil was a bright boy, fond of seeing what was going on; he watched the men at work, listened to

what was said about the different
horses, and so busied himself that
the time passed quickly.

2. It was after three o'clock when
Neil was ready to return home. Bay
Billy started off in fine style; he had
covered two miles, when Neil saw a
man lying on the ground near the
railroad station.

3. Getting off his horse, Neil hurried
to the man's help, but on reaching him
found he was in a drunken sleep, and,
much to the boy's surprise, that he was
the switchman, Leonard's father. Then
Neil remembered that some one in the
blacksmith's shop had said it was to be
hoped the switchman was all right to-
day, as there were so many extra trains,
he would need all his wits.

4. What was to be done? It was
impossible to rouse the man; Neil
could not tell whether or not the
switch was right, and the train that
carried his father and hundreds of
others might be along at any moment.
There was no time to lose if a wreck
was to be prevented. Mounting Bay

Billy, Neil rode with all haste to a little hill, which overlooked the track.

5. With the keen edge of his freshly
sharpened hatchet, it was the work of a
few minutes to cut a long branch
from a tree, to which he attached his red and black tennis
coat; then remounting
the horse, he

waited
for the
train.

6. As it came in sight, Bay Billy
reared and plunged, but his young
master held him in check with one
hand, while with the other he waved
aloft the danger signal and shouted to
the engineer. Then came a sharp
whistle, Neil saw the train-men tug-

ging at the brakes, the speed grew less and less, and finally the train came to a stop.

7. In a few minutes, the brave boy was in his father's arms. Later on, when all danger was past, the passengers were forcing on Neil a gift of money, while his father looked on, not knowing what to do. "What can such a boy do with money?" he asked. "He has no wants."

8. "Do with it?" roared a wealthy farmer, who, with his son, had been on the train. "Do with it? Let him buy peanuts with it, if there is nothing else he wants; but do not deprive us of the pleasure of showing we are grateful to one who has saved our lives. What is such a poor, mean thing as money compared to the lives of those we love?"

So the doctor had to give in.

9. That night, when talking over the events of the day, Neil said "I suppose, father, I can use part of my present for a bicycle?"

"No, my boy," said the doctor. "Put the money in a bank. I do not believe

in rewards for merely doing your duty.
As to the bicycle, I mean to buy one for
you myself, because I think you have
earned it. You lost your holiday, but
you knew your duty and did it."

Language Lesson.

What is meant by the following expressions?
"To rouse the man"; "if a wreck was to be prevented"; "held him in check"; "tugging at
the brakes"; "what is such a poor, mean thing
as money, compared to the lives of those we
love?" "the events of the day."

LESSON XLIV.

bŭb'blĕ'	worth'lesş	păl'a-ta-blĕ
nā'tionş	(wûrth'lesş)	tĕs'ta-ment
ob-tāin̯ĕd'	ne-çĕs'si-tў	frē'quent-lў
pre-şĕrv'ing		mĭs'sion-a-rĭeş

Salt.

1. Salt is as necessary as bread or
meat. Without it neither the one nor
the other would be palatable. Salt, like
water, is used by rich and poor, by man
and beast. Like water, too, it is found
almost everywhere.

2. In some places, salt is dug out of
the earth from mines, like coal or iron;
this is called "rock salt." In other

places, there are springs of salt water
that bubble out of the earth; this water
is led into large pans which are placed
over a fire, when the water passes off
in steam, and the salt remains in the
pan; this is called "spring salt." One
of the first salt springs known in this
country was discovered in the State of
New York by the early Catholic mis-
sionaries.

3. There is another kind of salt
known as "sea salt," which is obtained
from sea water. This is used largely for
pickling and preserving fish and meats.
It is purer than spring salt, which often
contains lime.

4. The uses of salt have been known
from the earliest times; it is frequently
spoken of in the Old Testament. Even
among savage nations salt is regarded
as a necessity. In some parts of Africa,
on the Gold Coast, for example, salt was
so prized that a handful of it was considered next in value to gold, and men
were formerly sold for it: a brother
would sell his sister, a husband his
wife, parents their children. With us,

salt is so cheap that we say of a worth-
less fellow, "He is not worth his salt."

Language Lesson.

Learn the singular and the plural form of the following:

man	mouse	ox	tooth
men	mice	oxen	teeth
brother	child	foot	goose
brethren	children	feet	geese

LESSON XLV.

ea'ger	brä'voṣ	Whĭt'sun
braĭdṣ	hĕr'aldṣ	mĭn'er-al
drĭlled	twĭṇk'le	mŏn'areḥ
naŭght	grā'cioŭs	eăv'al-eāde'
eŏnned	drĕad'ful	hĕnçe-fŏrth'

Little Christel.

1. Fräulein, the young schoolmistress, to
    her pupils said one day,
  "Next week, at Whitsun holiday, King
    Ludwig rides this way;
  And you will be wise, my little ones, to
    work with a will at your tasks,
  That so you may answer fearlessly what-
    ever questions he asks.
  It would be a shame, too dreadful, if the
    king should have it to tell
  That Hansel missed in his figures and
    Peterkin could not spell."

2. "Oho! that never shall happen," cried
Hansel, and Peterkin too;
"We'll show King Ludwig, when he
comes, what the boys in this school
can do."
"And we," said Gretchen and Bertha,
and all the fair little maids
Who stood in a row before her, with
their hair in flaxen braids,
"We will pay such good attention to
every word you say
That you shall not be ashamed of us
when King Ludwig rides this way."

3. She smiled, the young schoolmistress, to
see that they loved her so,
And with patient care she taught them
the things it was good to know.
Day after day she drilled them till the
great day came at last,
When the heralds going before him, blew
out their sounding blast;
And with music and flying banners, and
the clatter of horses' feet,
The king and his troops of soldiers rode
down the village street.

4. O! the hearts of the eager children
beat fast with joy and fear,
And Fräulein trembled and grew pale as
the cavalcade drew near;

But she blushed with pride and pleasure
when the lessons came to be heard,
For in all the flock of the boys and girls
not one of them missed a word,
And King Ludwig turned to the teacher
with a smile and a gracious look,
"It is plain," said he, "that your scholars
have carefully conned their book.

5. "But now let us ask some questions, to
see if they understand:"
And he showed to one of the little maids
an orange in his hand.
It was Christel, the youngest sister of the
mistress, fair and kind—
A child with a face like a lily, and as
lovely and pure a mind.
"What kingdom does this belong to?"
as he called her to his knee;
And at once—"The vegetable," she answered quietly.

6. "Good," said the monarch, kindly, and
showed her a piece of gold;
"Now tell me what this belongs to,—the
pretty coin I hold."
She touched it with careful finger, for
gold was a metal rare,
And then—"The mineral kingdom," she
answered with confident air.
"Well done for the little maiden!" And
good King Ludwig smiled

At Fräulein and her sister, the teacher
and the child.

7. "Now answer me one more question "—
   with a twin-
   kle of fun
   in his eye:
   "What king-
   dom do

I belong to?" For he thought she
   would surely reply,
"The animal;" and he meant to ask,
   with a frown, if that were the thing
For a little child like her to say to her
   lord and master, the king.
He knew not the artless wisdom that
   would set his wit at naught,
And the little Christel guessed nothing
   at all of what was in his thought.

8. But her glance shot up at the question,
and the brightness in her face,
Like a sunbeam on a lily, seemed to
shine all over the place,
"What kingdom do you belong to?" her
innocent lips repeat;
"Why, surely, the kingdom of Heaven!"
rings out the answer sweet.
And then for a breathless moment a
sudden silence fell,
And you might have heard the fall of
a leaf as they looked at little Christel.

9. But it lasted only a moment, then rose
as sudden a shout—
"Well done! well done for little Christel!" and the bravos rang about.
For the king in his arms had caught her,
to her wondering shy surprise,
And over and over he kissed her, with a
mist of tears in his eyes.
"May the blessing of God," he murmured, "forever rest on thy head!
Henceforth, by His grace, my life shall
prove the truth of what thou hast
said."

10. He gave her the yellow orange and the
golden coin for her own,
And the school had a royal feast that

To Fräulein, the gentle mistress, he
spoke such words of cheer
That they lightened her anxious labor
for many and many a year.
And because in his heart was hidden
the memory of this thing,
The Lord had a better servant, the people a wiser king!

Language Lesson.

What proper noun in the first stanza means "Pen-
tecost"? What word in the fourth stanza
means "studied"?

Explain the meaning of "heralds"; "sounding
blast"; "the *cavalcade* drew near"; "set his
wit at naught"; "*bravos* rang about."

*Point out all the proper names in the lesson. Afterward,
tell the story of the poem in your own language.*

LESSON XLVI.

slīght	sē'ri-ǫŭs	stŏǫk'ings
flăx'ẹn	Frăn'çeş	su-pē'ri-or
Te-rē'så	re-prōōf'	ġĕn'er-ŏs'i-tў

Florence.

1. Florence was a pupil at St. Mary's
Convent School. She was about twelve
years old: generous, kind-hearted, and
full of fun, but always getting into
scrapes. It must be said in her favor,
however, that, no matter how much she

was to blame, or what the result might be, she always told the truth.

2. One day, when the scholars were in the beautiful garden that was used for a playground, Florence was missing. Search was made for her, and at last Sister Frances heard a voice overhead, and looking up, saw Florence sitting on the garden wall, talking to some one on the other side.

"Florence," called out the Sister, "come down." The voice was sharp and sudden; it made Florence start and lose her balance, so, instead of coming down as she was told, she fell on the other side of the wall.

3. When the gate was opened, she stood holding the hand of a poor, little barefooted child. As an apology for her conduct, Florence said, "I heard this little girl crying, so I climbed to the top of the wall to learn what was the matter, and I found that she had broken her doll."

"Leave the child to me," said Sister Frances, "and go to the Mother superior and show her your dress."

4. Mother Teresa knew the girl's heart, and loved her though she was always breaking the rules. So, when Florence entered, with her dress torn, the good Mother could hardly keep from smiling. After a slight reproof, and some questions about the poor child and her broken doll, Mother Teresa asked, "Would you like to give that barefooted child a pair of shoes and another doll?"—"O, yes!" exclaimed Florence, "please let me. I will be ever so good, and never climb the wall again."

5. "Very well. Could you deny yourself in order to help the child? I do not mean by giving money. There are more difficult ways to deny one's self. Could you keep the rules for a week to get that barefooted child a pair of shoes and a doll?"—"Indeed, I could. At least I would try very hard."

6. That was a long week for Florence. There were so many rules, and they were so easily broken; but, at last, the end of the week came. It was a sunny summer day when Florence ran down

to the gate-house, and there found her poor little friend eating a slice of bread and jam. Sister Frances was there, too, and on a table was a large doll, with flaxen hair and blue eyes, and a pink dress dotted with silver stars.

"O, how lovely!" cried Florence. "See," she said to the child, "what a beautiful doll the Sisters have given me for you! Be careful you do not get jam on it." The child stood looking on without a word, but when Florence placed the doll in her arms she burst into a laugh of gladness. She had received shoes and stockings, too.

7. Florence was happy, and as soon as the child had gone, she turned to Sister Frances, "Now, Sister," she said, "I must have some fun. O, you do not know how tied-up I have felt all the week! Here goes—" Her shoes went flying through the air, and she danced out into the garden. It happened that Mother Teresa was just passing, and Florence came face to face with her. "You are the very child I want," said the Mother, after listening to Florence's

apologies. "Put on your shoes, and walk round the garden with me."

8. That night Mother Teresa said, "Florence has faults, but not serious ones, and who knows but that generous soul may yet do great things. Some day, when she has forgotten about it, the great Lover of little children may remind her how she earned the shoes and the doll."

9. About ten years later, a lady who had been a pupil at the convent school received a call from two Sisters. They were collecting alms for the support of the orphans under their care. "We shall be thankful for anything, no matter how small," said one. "It is for our Lord, you know, and He will remind you of it some day, when you have forgotten it."

10. That sounded like Mother Teresa; the lady looked more closely at the Sister who had spoken, and there, under the black veil, she saw the happy face of an old friend. "Why, Florence, my dear Florence, how do you do?" she cried.

11. There was Florence, sure enough,

bright and smiling as ever. Her generosity had led her to give herself wholly
up to "keeping rules," for the sake of
the great Lover of children whom she
loved.

Language Lesson.

Explain the meaning of the following expressions :

"What the result might be"; "it must be said in
her favor"; "an apology for her conduct"; "a
slight reproof"; "could you deny yourself?"
"the great Lover of little children."

*Write the following words in the plural form by changing
f or fe to ves :*

calf	leaf	life	wife
half	knife	thief	wolf

LESSON XLVII.

sŭm′mit   con-tĕmpt′   pĕr′ishĕd
ĭm′mi-nent   lĭb′er-āt-ed

The Hero of Johnstown.

1. A hero is one who shows contempt
of danger in the performance of some
great or noble action. There have been
heroes in all ages and in all nations, but
none better deserves the name than one
of our own time and our own country.

2. On the summit of a hill which
overlooks a valley, there was a large
fish preserve, or pond, almost as large

as a lake. The wall of this pond had become weak in places, and at last giving way, the liberated water rushed

in a torrent down the hill. Bridges were destroyed, houses were carried away, and men, women, and children perished in the flood.

3. If an alarm could be given to those living within a short distance,

many might be saved; but at such a time every one thinks only of saving himself.

4. No, not every one. There was one man who thought of others. He was young and wealthy, with everything to make life happy. He saw the coming water, and knew the imminent danger. Springing to his horse, he galloped ahead, shouting to every one he met: "Fly for your life; the flood is coming!"

5. He could hear the water as it leaped nearer and nearer, but on, on he rode, thinking only of others, and caring nothing for his own safety, till at last he was overtaken and drowned.

6. That young man's name was Daniel Peyton, and he was quite as great a hero as Paul Revere. He should not be forgotten, for he gave his life to save others.

Language Lesson.

1. Write a composition suggested by the picture.
2. What famous hero of the Revolution does the picture recall? Who was Paul Revere?
3. What other words might be used instead of "contempt," "summit," "liberated," "per-

LESSON XLVIII.

hawk	roy'al	răp'id-ly̆
ăr'rōw	mō'tion	stiff'ĕn̆d
de-vour'	wĕap'on	sus-pĕnd'ed

Dictation Exercise.

The lion is called a *royal*, or kingly, animal.—Wild beasts *devour* their food, or they eat it greedily. —The man had no *weapon*, that is, nothing with which to defend himself.

The Humming-Bird.

1. The little humming-bird, which is one of the most beautiful of all creatures, is found only in America. Its feathers have all the colors of the rainbow, and are as bright as bits of polished metal. It receives its name from the humming or buzzing sound it makes with its wings, while suspended in air feeding from a flower.

2. The legs of this bird are weak and delicate, but the wings are remarkably strong, which shows that it is intended to pass more time in the air than on the ground. Even when feeding, the bird seldom stops to perch, but hangs suspended in the air. The sweet juices of flowers are its principal food,

but now and then it must have spiders and other insects, otherwise it would soon die.

3. When at full speed, the humming-bird flies so fast that the eye can not follow, and its wings move so rapidly that they look like small gray fans fastened to its sides. This tiny bird does not fear the eagle, hawk, or owl, which devour other small birds, for it knows they can not overtake it.

4. The beak of the humming-bird is long and thin, which enables the bird to reach the inner parts of the flowers. Its beak also serves as a weapon, and the brave little creature will resist any bird of prey that dares come too near its nest. It has been known to attack even the eagle, and, perched on the head of the royal bird, to peck away, and scatter the feathers right and left.

5. The humming-bird can not stand the cold, and if kept from sunlight it will soon droop and die. A gentleman who kept a humming-bird in a cage placed it in a shaded part of the room. The weather was cold, and after awhile

the little creature stiffened out, and
seemed to be dead. It did not appear to
breathe, the eyes were shut, and, when
touched by the finger, it gave no signs
of life or motion.

6. The gentleman carried it into the
open air, and placed it in the sun. In
a few seconds, it began to breathe,
opened its eyes, and soon appeared to
be as lively as ever. After it had come
to, it flew to the top of a tree, where it
sat for some time, dressing its feathers,
and then shot off like an arrow.

Language Lesson.

What is meant by the following expressions?
"hangs suspended in the air"; "they can not
overtake it"; "resist any bird of prey"; "gave
no signs of life or motion"; "dressing its
feathers."

*Write the plural form of the following words which end in
y, preceded by a consonant, by changing the y into
i, and adding es.*

baby	body	copy	story
army	cherry	lady	daisy

Memory Gems.

He that feasts till he is sick, must fast till he is
well.

Never put off till to-morrow what can be done
to-day.

e to your

e to you

my regards

s of *your*

friend,

Sara.

on.

e letter as you think
declining with regret,

following words and
s been so occupied";
ght."

L.

dĕd'i-eāt-ed
eon-çĕp'tion
as-sŭmp'tion
pŏv'er-ishĕd

s.

red **years ago, one**
tains was Christo-
pious and learned
ges and stud d
t the earth is

seemed to be a pleasant, amiable girl. Her death must be a great blow to her parents. May she rest in peace. Please say to her parents that they have my deepest sympathy.

Now, Agnes, I want you to promise that you will come and spend some months with us. Mother is very anxious that you should come, and I shall take no excuse. My uncle will go East on business in a fortnight; he will return about the first week in October, and I hope you will make up your mind to come with him. There is so much here that I would like to show you.

Write as soon as you receive this, and let me know when I may expect you.

Please remember me to your dear parents. With love to you and your sister, and my regards to the other members of your family, I am

Your sincere friend,

Sara.

Language Lesson.

Write such an answer to the above letter as you think Agnes wrote, accepting, or declining with regret, Sara's invitation.

Explain the meaning of the following words and expressions: "My time has been so occupied"; "a great *blow*"; "a fortnight."

LESSON L.

ĭ-dē'ăş	Ĭş'a-bĕl'lȧ	dē'di-eāt-ed
voy'aġ-eş	rĭd'i-eūlȩd	eon-çĕp'tion
ăd'mi-rals	e̱x-hȧu̇st'ed	as-sŭmp'tion
eom-mūn'ion		im-pŏv'er-ishȩd

Columbus.

1. About four hundred years ago, one of the greatest sea-captains was Christopher Columbus, a pious and learned Italian. His voyages and studies led him to believe that the earth is round,

though, at that time, it was generally thought to be flat. Columbus also believed that by sailing west from Europe he could reach India, and he was anxious to make such a voyage.

2. He spent all his money in preparing plans, and when his own means were exhausted he asked the government of different countries to help him, but they refused. His ideas were ridiculed. It was claimed that if the world were round people on the other side would be upside down and could not live, and some who thought themselves very wise said that while a ship might sail *down* the sides of the world, it would be impossible to get back *up* again.

3. Poor and friendless, leading his little son by the hand, Columbus one day knocked at the door of a Franciscan convent, in Spain, to ask for food and shelter. He was worn out, and the good friars bade him stay and rest. Columbus did so, and was made so welcome that he remained there nearly a year. While at the convent, he became intimately acquainted with the Guardian,

or superior, who had formerly been the confessor of Queen Isabella of Spain.

4. The Guardian was a learned man, and when he had examined the plans of Columbus he agreed with the captain's views, and gave him letters to the Queen, who, in turn, became greatly in-

terested. Though her country was impoverished by war with the Moors, Queen Isabella furnished the daring sailor with money. In a short time, Columbus had three small vessels at his command, and on the morning of August 3, 1492, having heard Mass and received holy Communion, he set sail.

5. When the vessels had been at sea
for several weeks without any signs of
land appearing, the crew became frightened and began to rebel, and even
threatened to throw Columbus over-
board and return. He kept up their
courage by every means in his power,
even by concealing from them how far
they had come.

6. The hand of Heaven was guiding
Columbus, however; one night he saw
a light, and at two o'clock the following
morning, which was October 12, 1492,
land was sighted. The joyful crew fell
at their captain's feet, to show their
reverence; but he fell on his knees to
praise and thank Almighty God. Columbus believed that this land was India, but it afterward proved to be a "new
world." Thus was America discovered.

7. Like all pious men, Columbus had
a great devotion to the Blessed Virgin.
His first ship was called *Santa Maria.*
It was in a chapel dedicated to the
Mother of God that he and his crew
received holy Communion before starting on their voyage, and every evening

a hymn to Mary was sung on the three ships.

8. When land was discovered, Columbus named many places in honor of the Blessed Virgin. On his second voyage to America he called the admiral's ship *Gracious Mary;* and on his third voyage he named the first island he met *Conception* and another *Assumption,* and now that he is enjoying his reward in heaven, his bones rest in the chapel of the Immaculate Conception in Havana.

Language Lesson.

1. How long is it since Columbus discovered America?
2. Who assisted Columbus by giving him letters to Queen Isabella?
3. On what day was America discovered?

Change the form of the action-word, or verb, in the following sentences, so that it will mean the present time:

"One of the greatest sea-captains *was* Christopher Columbus"; "he *spent* all his money"; "his ideas *were* ridiculed"; "some who *thought* themselves very wise *said* it would be impossible to get back again"; "he *agreed* with the captain's views."

Memory Gem.

Honor and fame from no condition rise ;
Act well your part; there all the honor lies.

LESSON LI.

beau'te-ous   re-flĕct'ed   rā'di-ançĕ
rĕc'om-pĕnsĕ   ŭn-de-fīlĕd'

Loveliness.

1. Once I knew a little girl
    Very plain ;
You might try her hair to curl,
    All in vain ;
On her cheek no tint of rose
Paled and blushed, or sought repose ;
    She was plain.

2. But the thoughts that through her brain
    Came and went,
As a recompense for pain,
    Angels sent ;
So full many a beauteous thing,
In her young soul blossoming,
    Gave content.

3. Every thought was full of grace,
    Pure and true,
And in time the homely face
    Loveliest grew,
With a heavenly radiance bright,
From the soul's reflected light,
    Shining through.

4. So I tell you, little child,
    Plain or poor,

You are sure
Of the loveliness of worth;
And this beauty, not of earth,
Will endure.

Language Lesson.

Who is the subject of this poem? Explain in your own language the meaning of the three last lines of the second stanza. What resulted from the purity of the girl's thoughts? What is meant by "the loveliness of worth"?

LESSON LII.

fẽrnṣ	eär'bon	dī'a-mondṣ
oͅz'eṣ	pẽr'fūmeͅṣ	wĭl'der-nesͅ
gḣōsts	plĕn'ti-fuͅl	un-dis-tûrbͅd'
	ex-trăet'ed	noͅͅ ͏ŭr'ish-ment

Coal.

1. On a winter day, as you stand before a bright fire warming your fingers, do you ever consider where the coal comes from that throws out so much heat? You know, perhaps, that it is dug out of a mine, but if asked what coal is, you would probably say it is a kind of stone that burns.

2. It looks like stone, it is true, but coal is made of the leaves, stems, and

into a hard mass by the weight of the
rocks that for thousands of years have
gathered over them. All coal once grew
as mighty forests, many of whose trees
must have been taller than ours are at
present. The ferns of those days were
very plentiful, and were not the humble
plants they are now. The woods were
a dark green wilderness undisturbed by
man, for this happened long before man
was created.

3. Think how many years it must
have taken to grow enough flowers and
leaves and trees to make all the coal
there is, and how much of the sun-
shine of that time must be shut up in
the black lumps we burn.

4. Coal is often called "black diamonds," for both coal and diamond are
composed of what is known as carbon.
The diamond is pure carbon; it sparkles
with the colors of the rainbow, while
coal is dull and lifeless. But throw a
lump of coal on the fire, and we shall
see leaping from it flames of red and
yellow, ghosts, perhaps, of the sun-
beams which gave light and warmth

and nourishment to the plants from which coal comes.

5. From coal we get the gas that is used to light our houses; nor is this the last of the wonders of a piece of coal. From the tar that oozes out of the heated mass are extracted the most delicate shades of red, blue, green, and yellow to be found in the ribbons, silks, and other stuffs worn by women and girls. Some of the sweetest perfumes we have are made from this coal-tar, which might lead us to imagine that the fragrant scent of the flowers lay hidden in the coal, till brought out by the skill of man.

6. What a wonderful substance coal is! It furnishes us not only with heat and light, but with delicate colors and refreshing perfume.

Language Lesson.

Write a composition on *coal;* tell where it comes from, of what it is made, and any other facts you know relating to it.

Memory Gems.

Sloth is the mother of poverty.
Many hands make light work.

Familiar Talks on Common Things.

INDIA-RUBBER.—What is India-rubber? India-rubber is the sap of a tree that grows in South America.

How is the sap obtained from the tree? The sap is obtained by making holes in the bark, through which the sap runs into clay cups or shells placed ready to receive it.

What is the sap like as it comes from the tree? The sap is like a milky juice, and hardens in the air.

What is done to the sap afterward? The sap is moulded into bottles of a pear shape, and passed through the smoke of a palm-nut fire.

For what is India-rubber remarkable? India-rubber is water-proof, and very elastic.

Why is it called rubber? It is called *rubber* because one of its earliest uses was to *rub* out pencil-marks.

To what other uses is it now put? Coats, shoes, and caps are made of India-rubber; as well as combs, trays, and a great many ornaments.

CORK.—What is cork? Cork is the outer bark of a kind of oak-tree.

Where does the cork-tree grow? The cork-tree grows in Spain, France, Italy, and the north of Africa.

How is cork gathered? To gather cork, the whole trunk is skinned of its bark once in every eight or ten years; for if the inner bark is uninjured, the outer bark grows again.

For what is cork remarkable? Cork is very light, elastic, and proof against most liquids.

For what is cork used? Cork is used for making stoppers of bottles, net-floats, life-buoys, lining of shoes, and many other things.

CORAL.—What is coral? Coral is a horny or stony substance, formed by little sea-insects on rocks and shoals.

Where is coral found? Coral is found in the Mediterranean and in the Pacific Ocean.

What is coral like? Coral has many stems and branches, and looks like groups of bare trees.

What is a coral-reef? A coral-reef is a vast mass of coral, extending sometimes for hundreds of miles.

What islands were originally coral-reef? Many of the South Sea Islands were originally coral-reef.

How is coral obtained? Coral is obtained in the same way as sponge—by diving.

The foregoing will suggest fruitful themes for composition, and also be useful as a dictation exercise.

LESSON LIII.

sŭlk′ў   här′nесsĕd   sĭm′i-lar
mŭz′zlᴇ   Ĕs′qui-maux   pătk′aġ-eş
slăᴄk′ᴇn   (ĕs′kĭ-mōz)   prŏs′per-ᴏ̆ŭs
      rᴇin′deer   ex-pē′ri-ençᴇ

The Reindeer and the Esquimau Dog.

1. In the extreme northern part of Europe is Lapland, a country of ice and snow, where for many months of the year the sun is never seen. The Laplanders, or Lapps, as the natives are called, dwell in huts built of mud or in tents made of hides. and their greatest

happiness is to own
a number of reindeer,
which they value as we
value money.

2. The Lapp who owns a thousand
reindeer is looked upon as rich; he
who has only a few hundred is well
off; while the owner of forty or fifty is
considered poor, and acts as a servant
to his more prosperous. countryman,
keeping his little herd with the larger
herd of his employer.

3. To the Lapp the reindeer is as
useful as the horse, the cow, or the ox
is to us, but, unlike those animals, it
requires little care, for it lives out-
doors in the coldest weather, not seek-
ing shelter of any kind. Its food con-

sists principally of a moss, which, even when buried deep under the snow, the reindeer will scent out and lay bare by scraping away the snow with its head, hoof, and snout.

4. The milk of the reindeer is good and rich, and from it the Lapp makes excellent cheese. In midwinter, when fish can not be caught, and the wild fowls have flown to warmer climates, the reindeer's flesh serves for food, while its skin makes clothes and tents.

5. The reindeer is valuable as a beast of burden; it draws the sled and carries men and packages over the snow, at the rate of nine or ten miles an hour. The deer is harnessed to the sled by a strap which passes under its body, and is fastened to a collar at its neck. The sled is shaped much like a boat, and the Lapp sits against its back with his legs stretched out on the bottom.

6. A ride in a reindeer sled is not as comfortable as in a railroad car. It is rapid traveling, but till the driver has had some practice he is likely to

be pitched head foremost into the snow. On a long journey, the reindeer may give out, in which case the driver's skates are his only hope, and if these fail him, he will die in the snow or be devoured by wolves.

7. What the reindeer is to the Laplanders the dog is to the Esquimaux, a people who inhabit the far North of America. The climate there is similar to that of Lapland; for the greater part of the year the ground is covered with ice and snow.

8. The Esquimau dog somewhat resembles a wolf. It has a long muzzle, short, pointed ears, and a bushy tail, curling up over the back. Its life is passed in drawing sleds and carrying heavy loads, it being the only beast of burden in the extreme northern parts of America. In summer, some of the dogs are turned loose to get their own living, but most of them are kept at work, and these fare better than the others, for their work is not so heavy as in winter, and their food is much better.

9. When harnessed to a sled, the dogs follow their leader, a dog of experience. This dog knows the driver's voice, and will dash forward, slacken speed, and halt, or turn right or left at command. There are no means of guiding the animals except by the whip and the voice of the driver, for each dog is tied to the sled merely by a strap. It is, however, more the sound of the whip than the stroke, for the lash seldom touches a dog, as it is apt to cause a general fight, in which the sled is likely to be upset. Sometimes, a dog becomes offended at its fellows, the driver, or the road, and turning sulky, will stop; in such cases scarcely any punishment will make it move.

10. The Esquimau dog can travel long distances over the snow, and it has been known to make daily journeys of sixty miles for several days in succession.

Language Lesson.

Write a composition in which the reindeer and the Esquimau dog are compared.

Explain the meaning of "more prosperous countryman"; "will scent out"; "a beast of burden."

LESSON LIV.

thĭef	a-mĕndş'	grȧsp'ing
lĭn'ing	re-vēặlĕd'	ad-mīrĕd'
môr'sel	tĕmpt'ing	in-jŭs'tĭçę
ĭn'va-lĭd	ĭn'ti-matę	sus-pĭ'cioŭs

The Lost Ring.

1. Many years ago, there lived in France an officer who was known to be both brave and honest. He was very poor, but he concealed his poverty even from his intimate friends. His only daughter had long been an invalid, but he was unable to buy her any but the plainest food.

2. One feast day, his general invited him to a grand dinner given in honor

things served at dinner were some roast birds. The officer looked at the one placed before him, but though it was tempting he could not eat it, for he thought of his sick girl at home, and of how much good such a delicate morsel would do her. Then he asked himself, "Why not take it to her? It is mine." So, when no one was looking, he wrapped the bird in his clean handkerchief, and slipped it into his pocket.

3. After dinner, the general showed his guests a beautiful ring which had been presented to him; it was passed from one to the other and greatly admired. Later on, when the general asked for the ring, it could not be found, though none of the company would admit he had it.

4. "Let us be searched," said one. To this all agreed except the officer. He knew that if this were done the bird would be found in his pocket, and his poverty would be revealed. "You will have to take my word for it that *I* have not the ring," said he, "for I will not allow any one to search me."

5. Of course, this looked suspicious, and when the company separated soon afterward, every one believed the officer to be a thief. The story of the missing ring became known, and in a short time the suspected man found himself deserted by all his friends.

6. About a year had gone by, when, one day, as the officer was sitting alone in his house, thinking over his troubles, the general entered. "My dear fellow," he said, grasping his friend by the hand, "I come to make what amends I can for the great wrong done you. The missing ring is found. It had slipped into the lining of my coat pocket, where it has just been discovered. But I cannot understand why, knowing yourself to be innocent, you would not allow some one to search you the night of the dinner."

7. When the general learned the reason, his heart was touched. Then he gave a second dinner to which he invited all who had been at the first; and before the whole company he explained how the missing ring was found, and

what great injustice they had done a
noble man.

Language Lesson.

Fill the blanks with the proper name-words, quality-words, and action-words.

He was very poor, but he . . . . his . . . .
    even from his . . . . friends.
He was unable to buy her any but the . . . .
    food.
Among other . . . . things was a . . . . . bird.
He . . . . . . the bird in his . . . . handkerchief.
"My dear friend," he said, ... the . . . .
    by the hand.

Explain what is meant by the following expressions:

"*Intimate* friends"; "an *invalid*"; "it was *tempt-ing*"; "*delicate morsel*"; "greatly *admired*";
"his poverty would be *revealed*"; "looked *sus-picious*"; "*deserted* by his friends"; "*grasping*
the officer by the hand"; "make what *amends* I
can"; "what great *injustice* they had done."

LESSON LV.

shrĭlł	ex-ạlt′	a-flãmĕ′
äy ⍨	€loy′ing	ăn′gri-lў
chärm	mūş′ing	chăn′nels
speech	ab-sûrd′	stę̆d′fȧst
shrĭĕks	drę̆m′ў	o€-eā′şions

The King's Daughters.

1. The king's three little daughters, 'neath
    the palace windows straying,

Had fallen into earnest talk that put an
    end to playing,
And the weary king smiled once again to
    hear what they were saying.

2. "It is I who love our father best!" the
    eldest daughter said ;
  "I am the oldest princess!" and her
    pretty face grew red.
  "What is there none can do without ?—
    I love him more than—bread!"

3. Then said the second princess, with her
    bright, blue eyes aflame,
  "Than bread? A common thing like
    bread! Thou hast not any shame!
  Glad am I that I, not thou, am called by
    our mother's name.

4. "I love him with a better love than one
    so tame as thine ;
  More than—O, what, then, shall I say
    that is both bright and fine,
  And is not common? Yes, I know—I
    love him more than wine!"

5. Then the youngest of the daughters,
    whose speech would sometimes halt,
  For her dreamy way of thinking, said,
    "You are both in fault ;
  "'Tis I who love our father best—I love
    him more than salt!"

6. Shrill shrieks of merry laughter greeted
    her earnest word,
   And the two joined hands, exclaiming,
    "But this is most absurd !"
   And the king, no longer smiling, was
    grieved at what he heard,

7. For the little, youngest daughter, with
    her eyes of steadfast gray,
   Could always move his tenderness, and
    charm his care away.
   "She grows more like her mother dead,"
    he whispered, "day by day.

8. "But she is very little, and I will find
    no fault
   That while her sisters strive to see who
    most shall me exalt,
   She holds me nothing dearer than a
    common thing like salt."

9. The portly cook was standing in the
    courtyard by the spring ;
   He winked and nodded to himself : "That
    little quiet thing
   Knows more than both the others, as I
    shall show the king."

10. That afternoon at dinner there was
    nothing fit to eat ;
   The king turned, frowning angrily, from

And he found a cloying sweetness in the
dishes that were sweet.

11. "And yet," he muttered, musing, "I
can not find the fault;
Not a thing has tasted like itself but this
honest cup of malt."
Said the youngest princess, shyly, "Dear
father, they need salt."

12. A sudden look of tenderness shone on
the king's dark face,
As he sat his little daughter in the dead
queen's vacant place;
And he thought, "She has her mother's
heart—ay, and her mother's grace.

13. "Great love through smallest channels
will find its surest way;
It waits not state occasions, which may
not come, or may;
It comforts and it blesses hour by hour
and day by day."

Language Lesson.

*Copy the third, sixth, and ninth stanzas, and point out
the lines that end with similar sounds.*

Find other words to express the meaning of the
following: "'Neath"; "tame"; "halt"; "stead-
fast"; "exalt"; "portly"; "cloying"; "vacant"; "ay."

*Let three pupils commit to memory and recite stanzas 2,
3, 4, and 5, so as to impersonate the three princesses.*

LESSON LVI.

stū'por   ĕn'er-ġў   ex-prĕss&d'
Jĕṣ'u-it   glō'rĭ-ѻŭs   dĕl'ĭ-ea-çĭeṣ
bĭs'eҷit   re-prǫv'ing   Ѻär'tä-ġē'nä
thĭth'er   Na-tĭv'ĭ-tў   dis-eҷūr'aġ&d
  ҟnŏԝl'edġ&   ae-eŏm'pa-nĭed

Saint Peter Claver.

1. Three hundred years ago, the city of Cartagena was the great slave market of South America. Thither came, yearly, hundreds of vessels laden with men, women, and children who had been stolen from their homes in Africa, to be sold as slaves.

2. From the moment these poor people were taken prisoners till the vessels touched port, their lot was one of suffering and cruelty; but as soon as they reached Cartagena, they met a friend. This was Father Peter Claver, a holy Jesuit priest, who devoted his life to the unfortunate negroes. For thirty years he labored for these afflicted people, consoling and bringing them to a knowledge of God's truth. During that time, it is said, he had the happiness of bap-

tizing about four hundred thousand negroes.

3. His love for the slaves was so well known that, upon the arrival of a slave-ship, the pious people of the city hastened to gratify him by bringing him the news; for this he remembered them in his prayers. Providing himself with cooling drinks, fruit, biscuit, and other delicacies, the priest hurried to the unhappy blacks. Before they were ready to leave the ship, Father Claver was there to help them; he provided wagons to remove the sick, accompanied others to their new homes, and begged their masters to treat them kindly.

4. Having gained the love of the slaves, Father Claver instructed them in the truths of religion, neither discouraged by the stupidity of some nor the rough ways of others. Not content with making them Christians, he wanted them to be good Christians; to gain this end he continued to visit and instruct them, encouraging those who lived piously and reproving those who did wrong.

5. When not otherwise engaged, Father Claver spent his time in the hospital, tending the sick, dressing their wounds, and waiting on them as if he were their slave. In fact, he called

himself "The Slave of the Slaves." Nor were the negroes alone the objects of his care, for wherever God's work was to be done Father Claver was there to do it with energy and love.

6. For thirty-two years this holy priest labored among the poor, the

sick, and the neglected; then our Lord called him to his reward. For many months before his death he could not rise from his bed without help, and during that time he was often uncared for. Yet he never complained, though he sometimes expressed sorrow that he could not assist at Mass or visit the Blessed Sacrament. More than once, in trying to rise without help, he fell and bruised himself severely.

7. On Sunday, September 6, 1654, he was helped to church for the last time, and after Communion, as he was returning to his room, he passed the sacristy. "I am going to die," he said to the Brother, though he then seemed no nearer death than for months past. That night the Saint fell into a stupor, and on the feast of the Nativity of the Blessed Virgin, his soul passed to its eternal and glorious reward.

Language Lesson.

Put the right word in the right place.

great	A man may be noble though he be poor. No one is
large	a —— man because he has a —— fortune.
vain	We do not blame a man who is —— of his success
proud	so much as one who is —— of his learning.

love **like**	It has been wisely said that we may —— a friend though we do not —— his faults.
little **small**	I have —— fear that you will soon be able to master so —— a book.
aged **old**	Most of my —— friends are still young men; but I have lately become acquainted with a very —— man.
dwell **live**	I —— in an old house, in the same town in which my family has been accustomed to —— for generations.
bad **evil** **ill**	The duke is very ——. Report says that he has been a —— man; but there is good reason to hope that he has repented of his —— deeds.
taught **learned**	The master who —— me grammar was a clever man. I —— more from him than from any other teacher.
cure **remedy**	He has tried nearly every —— in existence; but no —— has yet been effected.
faded **withered**	A —— tree cannot be expected to revive; a —— one may recover.
faults **defects**	The —— in his education will not excuse the serious —— in his conduct.

LESSON LVII.

lĭb′er-tў en-grāv′er dĭs′-po-ṣi′tion
re-quĕst′ rĕf′er-enç-eṣ ĭn-ᴄon-vēn′i-ençᴇ

Applying for a Situation.

JAMESTOWN, January 6, 189—.

Dear Mr. Beach :

It has been settled that I am to leave school at Easter, and as my father is a poor man, I would like to secure a situation without delay.

I prefer to learn a trade, and as I have a taste for drawing and am of a patient disposition, I believe I would make a good wood-engraver.

We have very few friends in the city, but father has spoken of you so often, that I take the liberty of asking if you can obtain a situation for me. As references, I have letters from our pastor and from my teacher, both of whom have known me all my life.

Father sends his regards to you.

Hoping that my request will not inconvenience you, and anxiously awaiting a reply, I remain,

Respectfully yours,
MAURICE FIELDS.

Language Lesson.

Write a letter to a friend on the subject of a situation just secured.

LESSON LVIII.

ăn'vil	chĭş'el	brănd'new
shĕạrş	eärvĕd	trādĕş'men
rĕ-pâïr'	frĭngĕd	o-rĭg'i-nāt-ed

Dictation Exercise.

The baker placed the loaf on his *peel,* or long wooden shovel, and put it in the oven to bake. — The king was known everywhere for his *generosity,* or nobility of soul, which made him despise anything mean.

The Blacksmith's Apron.

1. Every one that has seen a blacksmith at his work knows that he wears

an apron that is slit, and often fringed at the bottom. The custom is said to have originated in the following way :

2. When Alfred the Great was king of England, on one occasion he called together the different tradesmen for the purpose of selecting a Trades-king. The blacksmith came, and brought his hammer and a horseshoe; the tailor brought his shears and a new coat; the baker, his peel and a loaf of bread ; the shoemaker, his awl and a pair of shoes; the butcher, his chopping-knife and a joint of meat; the mason, his chisel and a carved stone.

3. When the different kinds of work were shown, the new coat looked so beautiful that all the tradesmen, except the blacksmith, declared the tailor king, and he was so named by King Alfred.

4. This made the blacksmith angry. Closing his shop, he said he would show who was king. Shortly after, King Alfred's horse lost a shoe, and the other tradesmen, each in turn, tried to shoe the horse. They not only failed, but broke their tools, and, till these were

mended, were unable to go on with their work.

5. Then King Alfred ordered the blacksmith's shop to be broken open, so that his tools might be used. When this was done, the king tried to shoe his horse, the tailor tried to mend his shears, and the others to repair their tools. But it was in vain; the horse kicked the king, the tailor hit his fingers with the hammer, the fire would not burn, and everybody got in everybody's way. In the general confusion, the anvil was knocked over.

6. About this time, the blacksmith walked in, looking very angry. King Alfred made a humble bow, and said, "I now see how wrong I was to be led away by a handsome coat, and as I have changed my mind, I name the blacksmith king."

7. All the trades, except the tailor, then begged the blacksmith to mend their tools; so he shod King Alfred's horse, mended the tools of all who asked him, and, to show his generosity, made the tailor a brandnew pair of shears.

8. In honor of the new king, King Alfred gave a grand dinner, to which the other tradesmen were invited. The tailor, who was jealous of the blacksmith, crawled under the table, and while the others were enjoying themselves, slit the blacksmith's apron, and cut the lower edge into a fringe.

9. From that day, no blacksmith has ever worn an apron that is not slit.

Language Lesson.

1. Explain the meaning of: "it is said to have originated in the following way"; "tradesmen"; a tailor's "shears"; a "peel"; a "joint of meat"; a "carved stone"; an "anvil."

2. In what different ways can we show our generosity?

Memory Gems.

Be slow to promise but quick to perform.
Debt is the worst kind of poverty.

LESSON LIX.

häu̱nts	dis-gu̱ıṣ̱ᶓ′	ae-cŏst′ed
vĕn′om	re-bū̆kᶓd′	un-sŭl′lied

A Nursery Tale.

1. O! did you not hear in your nursery
   The tale that the gossips tell,
   Of the two young girls that came to
   drink

The words of the youngest were as sweet
  As the smile of her ruby lip,
But the tongue of the eldest seemed to
    move
  As if venom were on its tip!

2. At the well a beggar accosted them
  (A sprite in a mean disguise);
The eldest rebuked her with scornful
    brow,
  That brought tears in her sister's eyes.
Cried the Fairy, "Whenever *you* speak,
    sweet girl,
  Pure gems from your lips shall fall,
But whenever *you* utter a word, proud
    maid,
  From your tongue shall a serpent
    crawl!"

3. And have you not met those sisters oft
  In the haunts of the old and young?
The *first* with her pure and unsullied lip?
The *last* with her serpent tongue?
Yes—the *first* is Kindness, and diamonds
    bright
  On the darkest theme she throws;
And the *last* is Slander, leaving the slime
  Of the snake wherever she goes!

Language Lesson.

Let the teacher write one stanza of this poem on the black-board, omitting the last word of each line, and have the pupils supply the blanks.

LESSON LX.

elĕrks			af-fŏrd′			ad-vȧnçe′
Ūn′ion			dŏl′lars			sin-çēre′lȳ
		se-cūre′			Cŏŏp′er

The Answer to Maurice Fields' Letter.

NEW YORK, January 15, 189—.

My dear young Friend:

I was very glad, indeed, to hear from you, and as soon as I received your letter I made it my business to inquire what were your chances to learn wood-engraving. I find, however, that it is difficult to obtain such a position, and learners never receive wages. As you could not afford to take a situation of that sort, I looked for something else, and believe I have found just the place for you.

A friend in the South American trade wants a boy in his office. To one who suits him he will pay three dollars a week. I consider it a desirable place, as the one who gets it will gain a knowledge of many kinds of business. My friend takes a great interest in his clerks, and advances them as they deserve. In the evenings, if you wished, you could attend the free night-classes at Cooper Union, and there study wood-engraving. Should you decide to accept this position, write at once, so that I can secure it for you.

Present my respects to your father, and
believe me,

Sincerely yours,

JOHN BEACH.

Language Lesson.

Fill the blanks in the following statements.

It is difficult to . . . . . . such a . . . .
You could not . . . . . . to take a . . . . of
that sort.

LESSON LXI.

gĕrm	de-sīgnĕd′	dăn′de-lī′on
es-sĕn′tial	a-bŭn′dant	eon-vĕn′ient
eŏ′eŏą-nŭt	de-pŏs′i-ted	ăb′so-lūtę-lў

Seeds.

1. The object of the flower in a plant
is to form the fruit or seed. The seed is
the only part of the fruit that is abso-
lutely necessary for the growth of the
plant, and the essential part of a seed
is the germ it contains. The germ is a
little plant, lying snugly packed away
in the seed, ready to grow into a new
plant when the seed is sown. To produce, protect, and nourish this germ,
is the object of the flower, the fruit,
and the seed.

2. When a seed that has been sown

receives enough heat, light, and moisture, it swells a little, and the germ, gradually waking from its sleep, sends out a little shoot, which, growing downward, forms the root; another little shoot forces its way upward, to unfold into the stem and leaves. No matter in what position the seed is planted, the root always turns down and the stem always goes up. What causes this, no one knows; but it is easy to

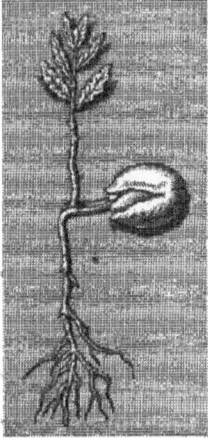

GERM, SHOWING THE GROWTH OF THE ROOTS AND THE STEM.

see why it should be so, since the dark, damp soil is the working place of the root, while the stem carries the leaves into the light and air, where they have their part to do in the growth of the plant.

3. At first, the young plant must be nourished by the seed, and on it the

PEACH PIT.

germ plant feeds and grows. In a peach pit, for example, the germ of the

little space within the shell, all the rest consisting of food designed for the nourishment of the young plant. This arrangement is still more easily seen in the cocoa-nut, where the true germ of the plant is a little point at one end, weighing only a few grains, while the rest of the nut, which is to supply the' nourishment, weighs many ounces.

4. The simple means provided for scattering seeds over the earth, and thus preventing the destruction of various kinds of plants, is very interesting. Many seeds are carried by the wind to places far distant from those in which they were produced. A well-known example of this is the dandelion. Its seed has a very light, downy

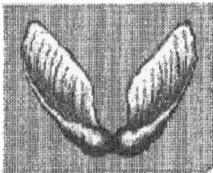

THE SEED OF THE
MAPLE.

covering, by which it is floated along by the slightest breath of air, till, by some cause it is deposited in the soil. The seeds of the maple are furnished with parts that spread out from the sides, and act as wings to bear them away.

5. Other seeds are conveyed by streams into which they fall and take root when left by the current on proper soil. Some seeds have a shelly or an oily covering that resists the action of the waters of the sea, and it is by this means that the coral islands of the Pacific are covered with an abundant growth of vegetation.

6. Floating branches of trees laden with their seeds are carried hundreds of miles by the tides and currents of the ocean; even gales and hurricanes lend their aid, and sow seeds on the ocean that take root and spring up on distant isles. Birds, too, take part in the dispersion of seeds. They carry off the whole fruit to a convenient place, and when they have eaten the pulp, the stone, which is useless to them, is dropped. The seed thus falls into the ground, and, in course of time, springs up a living plant. Squirrels, field-mice, and many other animals bury seeds in the ground, probably for the purpose of afterward feeding on them, and thus lead to the growth of plants and trees

in places where the seeds would not,
otherwise, reach.

What words can be used instead of "essential";
"deposited"; "vegetation"; and "dispersion"?

LESSON LXII.

whĭm	hăl′lōw	gŭĭlĕ′less
fẽr′tĭlĕ	tär′rĭed	brĕth′ren
re-trĕạt′	rŭs′tling	flŏŭr′ishĕd

The Child in the Midst.

1. There stood a stately convent,
   So olden legends run,
In a green and fertile meadow,
   Of which, when school was done,
The children made a playground,
   And frolicked in the sun.

2. But the old monks spoke complaining:
   "They drive all thought away;
In the woods the birds keep singing
   Throughout the live-long day,
And the laughter of the children
   Disturbs us when we pray."

3. Then spake the kind old abbot:
   "The woodland music sweet,
The sound of little voices,
   And the tramp of childish feet,
Are surely sent to gladden

4. "They bring with them a blessing,
    These happy, guileless things.
When I catch the children's laughter,
    Or when some small bird sings,
I think upon the angels,
    And hear the rustling wings.

5. "For myself, I love the children,"
    The abbot said and smiled,
"Amid a world of evil
    They as yet walk undefiled,
A likeness of the Savior
    Who for us became a child.

6. "I love to watch them flitting
    To and fro among the trees,
And to feel their clasping fingers
    As they cling about my knees;
And they who enter heaven
    Must be even such as these.

7. "He who 'suffered' little children
    Loves and watches o'er them still;
In the green and pleasant meadows
    They are safe from every ill;
Should we drive them hence, my breth-
    ren,
    Are we sure we do His will?

8. "Our eyes are often holden,
    Our sight is often dim,
Then bethink you well, my brethren,
    Lest through any foolish whim

In turning from the children
  We also turn from Him."

9. Then the brothers all made answer,
    As each sought his silent cell,
  "In the green and fertile pastures
    Christ's lambs shall surely dwell,

They are welcome, Father Abbot,
  For we see thou speakest well."

10. Long the song-birds sung and mated
    Beside the convent gray,
  And the old monks watched the children,
    And smiled upon their play,

Then found a double blessing
As they knelt to praise and pray.

11. And the convent grew and flourished
As a house of holy rest.
And with many a heavenly vision
Was the saintly abbot blest,
For the Lord who loves the children
Tarried always as his guest.

Language Lesson.

Say what other words could be used for the following: "fertile," "hallow," "guileless," "rustling,"
"undefiled," "holden," "whim," "tarried."

*Change the poetry into prose, and tell the story in your
own words.*

LESSON LXIII.

flight	yield'ed	sac'ri-fīce
re-lease'	plead'ed	as-sō'ci-āt-ed
ar-rears'	pe-tī'tioned	in-dŭs'tri-ous
con'victs	con-demned'	ŏp'por-tū'ni-tў

A Generous Convict.

1. In the prison at Brest, in France,
among the other convicts, there was a
quiet, hard-working young man named
Louis. He seldom associated with his
fellow-prisoners, and only spoke to
them in order not to appear unsociable.
He had been in the army, but one

fatal day thoughtlessly wandered from his regiment; he was arrested, tried as a deserter, and condemned to prison for six years.

2. Louis believed his sentence to be too severe, and, one stormy morning, early, he seized an opportunity to escape from prison. After wandering about the country for some hours, he ventured to approach a cottage, hoping to find food and rest.

3. On entering the cottage, a scene of great distress met him. Three little children were seated on the floor, in a corner of the room; their mother was crying as if her heart would break, while the father paced the floor, despair written on his face.

4. In answer to the inquiries of Louis, the father said, "You see before you a man without hope. I am in arrears for my rent, and unless I pay this morning what is due, my landlord will turn me out-of-doors, with my wife and little ones."

5. As Louis listened to the sad story, tears started to his eyes: all the ten-

der feelings of his heart were stirred.
He reflected for a moment, and then,
with a sudden resolution, said: "Courage, my friend. Listen to what I say.
I will give you the means to provide
for your family. I have just escaped
from prison, as you can see by my
clothes. Before long, my escape will be
discovered, and the guards will be on
my track. There is a reward of fifty
francs for the arrest of an escaped convict. Make haste to tie a rope around
me, and when the guards come, deliver
me up, and claim the reward."

6. "Never!" cried the man; "I could
not be so base."

"Think of your wife and children—"

"I would rather see them starve
than betray you."

7. At that moment, three reports of
a cannon were heard. "Hark!" said
Louis, "that is the signal that my flight
is known. Make haste, my friend, make
haste! If you do not consent to what
I propose, I will give myself up. Think
of your poor wife and helpless little

8. The generous convict pleaded so earnestly that the man at last yielded, and had just time to bind him with a rope when the guards entered.

9. The prisoner was taken back to the jail, and his captor received the fifty francs. As soon as the man had satisfied the debt due his landlord, he called on the prison chaplain, and in a voice broken by tears told him of the generous sacrifice Louis had made. The good priest listened with marked interest, and promised to see what could be done.

10. One evening, not long afterward, as the man whom Louis had saved was seated at home with his wife and children, the chant of a merry song reached their ears; the next moment Louis entered, and soon all were laughing and crying and talking by turns.

11. When the hand-shaking and embracing were over, Louis told the story of his release. The chaplain, moved by the heroic conduct of the soldier-convict, petitioned the government in his behalf. The case was examined, and

as the prisoner had served three years of his sentence, he was restored to liberty, in consideration of his noble sacrifice.

Language Lesson.

Write sentences which show that you know how to use the words which appear at the head of the lesson. Afterward, explain orally the meaning of the following words and expressions: "Associated with his fellow-prisoners"; "thoughtlessly wandered"; "condemned"; "despair written on his face"; "in arrears for rent"; "the tender feelings of his heart were stirred"; "a sudden resolution"; "pleaded"; "chant"; "petitioned the government in his behalf."

LESSON LXIV.

jŭn'glĕs   pär'a-sŏl'   fō'li-agĕ
seäf'fold   brĭll'iant   um-brĕl'lå
    trŏp'ie-al   länd'seāpĕ

Dictation Exercise.

In India, the *jungle,* that is, the land covered with forest trees and brushwood, is the home of the tiger and other wild beasts.—The hedge in our garden is a *compact,* that is, close, solid, mass of bushes.

The Bamboo.

1. One of the grandest sights in a tropical landscape is a clump or grove of bamboos. And yet the bamboo, with

its lordly height, and its feathery crown, is of the same family as the grass which we tread under our feet. It might almost be called a tree grass; for the stem, which in the grass is buried underground, rises in the bamboo, and forms a noble column, which has been compared to a pillar of a cathedral. The stem is hollow like that of the grass, and forms, at intervals, the same knots or joints.

2. In size the bamboo is more like the palm; it rears its stately head in the same majestic manner, crowned by a plume of feathery leaves of an emerald green. It may be called the tree of the tropics, for it grows everywhere within their range. In South America it forms dense jungles in the level country, and in the valleys of the Andes, and is considered next in value to corn and the sugar-cane.

3. Its home, however, is in India and China, and there it grows in all situations, on the banks of rivers and on the mountain heights. A hundred columns or stems will spring from a single

root, and rise to the height of a hundred feet.

4. Nothing can exceed the beauty of a thicket of bamboo. The traveler seems to be wandering through the arches of some mighty cathedral, built by the hand of nature. The stems are the columns, and the drooping branches form an intertwined roof more beautiful than can be described. Birds of brilliant plumage flit among the branches, and monkeys live as in a fairy bower.

5. The bamboo springs from the ground armed with a sharp point, which can force its way through the thickest mass of branches. The smooth stem mounts upward and upward, without sending any branch from its joints, until it has reached its full height.

6. Then, and not till then, the branches begin to spring ; at first smooth and without any shoots, until they have reached their utmost length. Thus, however numerous or delicate, they find no difficulty in piercing the dense growth. As each bamboo in the thicket sends out its shoots in this man-

ner, a compact mass of graceful foliage is formed by the countless branches crossing and recrossing one another.

7. The bamboo may be seen in the thicket in every stage of its growth. Pointed stems piercing through the tangled mass, tall stems of a clear yellow without any branches, and full-grown trees furnished with feathery plumes, as light and graceful as anything in nature.

8. There is a kind of bamboo with a stem that reaches a great height before it forms a single knot. This is just what the Indian wants to make the curious weapon he calls his blow-pipe. The blow-pipe is a long tube formed of two pieces of the hollow stem of the bamboo bound tightly together the whole length. It is a heavy weapon, and rather difficult to manage; but the Indian hunter contrives to bring down great quantities of game with it. He blows the arrows out of the upper end of the tube, and they wing their way in perfect silence.

think they were incapable of harming the smallest creature in the forest. They are made of the leaf-stalk of a species of palm, are small and slender, and have a sharp, needle-like point. This point, however, is dipped in one of those deadly poisons with which the Indian is familiar, and is as fatal as the fang of the rattlesnake.

10. Probably no other plant serves so many useful purposes as the bamboo. In India, China, and Japan, it supplies almost all the wants of life. The China-man not only constructs his house of bamboo, but all the furniture within it, even the bedsteads and bedding, is made of it. The sails, cables, and rig-ging of the junks, or vessels, that stud the rivers and canals are all made of bamboo.

11. The young shoots may be boiled for food or made into smooth, soft paper. The smaller stalks serve for walking-sticks, umbrella and parasol handles, stems of pipes, and various ornaments; whilst the larger stalks serve for drink-ing vessels, water-pipes, scaffold-poles,

or for making bridges. There is scarcely
any limit to the uses to which this
plant may be put.

Language Lesson.

Explain the words of similar sound but different meaning.

bored   Was it a carpenter that *bored* the hole in
board   that pine *board?*

haul   *Haul* that coil of rope into the *hall* of the
hall   new building.

hour   In an *hour*, it will be time for us to begin
our   *our* work.

need   We do not *need* the bread to-day; so I shall
knead   not *knead* the dough until to-night.

pane   The boy cut his hand with the broken *pane*.
pain   It caused him great *pain*.

LESSON LXV.

oys'ter   gŏg'glᴇ   lŏb'sters
spē'cial   eăv'erns   mûr'der-ᴏŭs

Some Wonders of the Sea.

1. If we could look into the depths
of the ocean, we would there behold
more strange sights and curious creatures than are to be found on land.

2. Darting about are fishes with
great goggle eyes, and mouths forever
opening and shutting; slimy sea-snails
and worms; great black and green lob-
sters with wicked-looking claws; tiny

crabs, some like small, hairy spiders, others like nothing but themselves; monstrous whales and swiftly. gliding, murderous sharks; shells of all shapes and sizes: some smooth, others spiny, still others curled and twisted like a spiral spring; many moving slowly hither and thither over the sands, rocks, and weeds; others lying motionless, the living creatures that inhabited them having perished.

3. Here are mountains and valleys, and deep caverns; forests of sea-weed, these of a dusky green, almost black, those bright as emerald; others crimson and pink; some with thick stems, like ropes; many like wisps of horse-hair, fine as the most delicate lace, spread over the rocks and sandy bottoms.

4. Here we have an oyster, not beau-tiful to look at, but with much to won-

are his special treasures. They are
caused in this way: worms bore through
the oyster's shell and hurt his body;
thereupon he throws on the injured
spot pearly matter, such as his shell
is lined with, and this soon becomes a
pearl of greater or less size. Sometimes
a grain of sand
gets into the
oyster's house,
and as that
hurts, he coats
it, too, with the
pearly matter.

5. That crab, creeping
sideways, lives in a hard
shell which never grows;
but as the crab grows he needs a new
home now and then. When obliged to
change his quarters, he creeps into some
hole that is safe. He then fasts till he
is so thin that his clothes hang about
him. In this state, a new, soft shell
forms around his body. A struggle follows, and the old shell being split, Mr.
Crab crawls out of it. He is no sooner

rapidly, and in a few days his new suit becomes as hard as his old one.

6. This star-shaped creature is known as the star-fish, and sometimes as five-fingers. Its mouth is in the very centre

of the rays, and though it has no jaws, it is a great devourer of shell-fish. A star-fish near an oyster-bed will do great damage, for in some way, not understood, it extracts the oyster from the shell and devours it.

7. That mass of jelly floating by is the sea-nettle, so called on account of the pain it causes when brought in contact with our skin. A delicate fringe, fine as a spider's web, trails from it, and with this the sea-nettle seizes its prey. If you take it alive, you will find you can not hold it, for it will divide into parts, and fall a shapeless mass.

8. Another wonder of the sea is the

but the lowest of all animals. It is pierced in all directions by canals from which streams of water are constantly discharged. It is supposed that the creature feeds on the water, and gets rid of it when it is drained of all nourishment.

9. These are but a few of the many wonders we would see could we walk open-eyed in the depths of the ocean.

Language Lesson.

Write a composition describing some of the wonders of the sea. Describe the shark, the swordfish, or any other submarine creature of which you have read or heard. Write about the diver who goes down to explore for sunken treasures, and tell of the curious sights he sees.

LESSON LXVI.

ca-rĕss'eş   com-pârĕd'
con-trĭv'ings   ăt'mos-phĕrĕ

Come To Me, O Ye Children.

1. What the leaves are to the forest,
     With light and air for food,
Ere their sweet and tender juices
     Have been hardened into wood—

2. That to the world are children;
     Through them it feels the glow
Of a brighter and sunnier climate

3. Come to me, O ye children!
   And whisper in my ear
   What the birds and the winds are sing-
     ing
   In your sunny atmosphere.

4. For what are all our contrivings
   And the wisdom of our books
   When compared with your caresses
   And the gladness of your looks?

5. Ye are better than all the ballads
   That ever were sung or said,
   For ye are the living poems,
   And all the rest are dead.

Language Lesson.

Change the following statement into a question.

   Ye are better than all the ballads
   That ever were sung or said.

Substitute other words or expressions for

"atmosphere," "contrivings," "ballads."

LESSON LXVII.

lĕdġe	em-ployĕd′	re-lī′a-bĭl′i-tў
jăg′ġed	prĕç′i-pĭç-eş	eon-grăt′ŭ-lātҽ
ehăşmş	eŏn′ti-nents	oe-eā′şion-al-lў

A Mule Ride in the Andes.

1. The Andes are a lofty mountain range stretching along the whole western coast of South America, from the

extreme south to the Caribbean Sea and the Isthmus of Panama. A continuation of the same vast range, known as the Rocky Mountains, extends along all the western part of North America to the Arctic Ocean, so that the Andes may be correctly described as the South American half of the wonderful mountain chain which runs through both continents. Some of the peaks rise to a height of more than 20,000 feet above the level of the sea, and one reaches even 23,910 feet.

2. The tops of the loftiest peaks are always covered with snow, even in tropical regions, and have never been reached by man. The whole range abounds in precipices, which sink down a thousand, or more, feet. Rapid rivers, called torrents, tumble down their sides, and in places there are perilous roads. The man or beast traveling over them needs a steady brain and a sure foot.

3. The mule is the animal employed to cross the Andes' roads, and he is remarkably suited for the difficulties

and dangers of the task. Let us each
mount one and prove this. Away we
go, with Indians for our guides. We
are not long on our way before we come
to roads as rough as stones can make
them; stones from the size of our fist
to the size of our body or the body of
our mule, smooth or jagged, and indeed
of every shape. They have been split
from the peaks by frost and have rolled
down to their base. Amid these our
mules skillfully find their way.

4. The rough road soon becomes
steep and winding. We look up and
wonder whether it is possible to go
farther, but the mules settle that question by plodding on. Hours pass, and
we begin to congratulate ourselves,
for the road ahead, though still steep,
promises to be smooth. Arrived at it,
however, we find that, though smooth
enough, it is only wet chalk, almost
as slippery as ice. The path, too, becomes narrower, and precipices are
nearer.

5. At the foot of these steeps, we have
to wait and let the Indian guides go on

to roughen the road, so as to make foot-
hold for the mules. This done, we are
off again.

6. Hitherto we have thought most
of the difficulty of our journey. Now
the only thought is its danger. Death
seems to stare us in the face every
moment. One false step of our mule,
and we would be dashed down a depth
the sight of which makes the brain reel.
Our mules occasionally tremble and
give a snort, which the guides tell us is
their way of saying "things look bad."

7. Our sense of insecurity is height-
ened by sitting on the mule's back.
We want to get down. We fancy we
should be safer on our own feet, but
our guides tell us there is no danger,
and entreat us to keep our seats, and
be sure to let the beasts have their
own way.

8. As we proceed danger increases.
Above us is a crag which rises, how
high we can not say, for we dare not
look, and below us another which sinks
to a depth we can not help seeing; for
the rock on which we are now is an

overhanging ledge. The path is not much wider than the seat of a chair, and between us and the dark torrent which runs five hundred feet below there is literally nothing. Holding our breath, we sit perfectly still, giving up the rein to the mule and ourselves to what appears certain death.

9. The top of the pass is finally gained; but before we have time to breathe we begin to go down on the other side. As we descend, the character of the upward road is repeated; now steep, narrow, rough; now smooth and slippery; then running among crags and chasms as before.

10. In the smooth, slippery, and steep parts, our wonderful beasts adopt an extraordinary method of motion. At the top of the incline they stand still, place their fore feet close together, and then their hind feet, bringing them quite near the fore ones. We think they are preparing to sit down to rest awhile. We soon find, however, that they are preparing to slide, for suddenly, with a

off we go down the road. It is marvelous how skillfully they steer themselves along, one after another sweeping round the bends of the road, inclining the body here slightly inward, and there slightly outward, now putting on a break with the hind feet, then taking it off again, and stopping themselves exactly when and where they desire.

11. When we have finished the long and difficult journey, we are of opinion that of all beasts of burden, for courage, trustiness, and skill, the mule must bear the palm.

Language Lesson.

Explain the meaning of the following words and expressions. "Mountain range"; "peaks"; "tropical regions"; "surmount"; "steep"; "plodding"; "congratulate"; "overhanging ledge"; "chasms."

Write a composition:

First, select the points of your subject.

Second, arrange them in order, and write them down in single words, as, for example: Subject: — *Snow*. Points: — (1) color, (2) cause, (3) season, (4) uses: (*a*) land, (*b*) fun.

Third, let the ideas on each point be clear.

Fourth, write one idea at a time.

Fifth, let each sentence be short.

LESSON LXVIII.

dạwn	ap-pēạl$̣s'$	sĕn'ti-ment
fĕr'vor	lăn'guagè	℮on-dĭ'tions
sўm'bol	quȧl'i-tĭe$̣$	hu-măn'i-tў
℈m'blem	hạẉ'thôrn	dis-tĭn'guishèd
im-ăg'i-nā'tion		pȧs'sion (pȧsh'un)

Dictation Exercise.

The crown is an *emblem,* or sign, of majesty, or royal power; the cross is the *symbol,* or sign, of our faith.

Flowers.

1. Flowers speak to the heart a language that appeals to every condition of life; they are full of instruction, and they cheer our pathway in life from childhood to old age.

2. If we watch a plant that is standing near a window, we shall find that its flowers turn toward the light. They will all face one way, if the pot remains in the same position; but by turning it a little every day, while the blossoms are opening, the plant can be made to show flowers on all sides.

3. In the greater number of plants flowering takes place, during the flowering season, at all hours of the day,

and the flowers, once opened, remain
open till they fade. Some, however,
shut themselves up at night, as if they
were going to sleep, and open again in
the morning. This is the case with the
sunflower, the tulip, and others.

4. A lady was one morning admir-
ing some flowers that had been sent
to her the evening before. Among
them were some tulips, and as one of
these opened, a bee flew out. He must
have been a lazy bee to be caught in
that way, when the flower was closing
for the night. Perhaps he had been
hard at work gathering honey, and became sleepy. At any rate, he stayed
too long in the tulip, and was kept a
prisoner there for the night.

5. The daisy is one of the flowers that
close at night; but it is as beautiful
and bright as ever when it awakes in
the morning. When it shuts itself up, it
forms a green ball, not unlike a pea,
and can hardly be distinguished from
the grass amidst which it lies. But in
the morning, the ball is open, showing

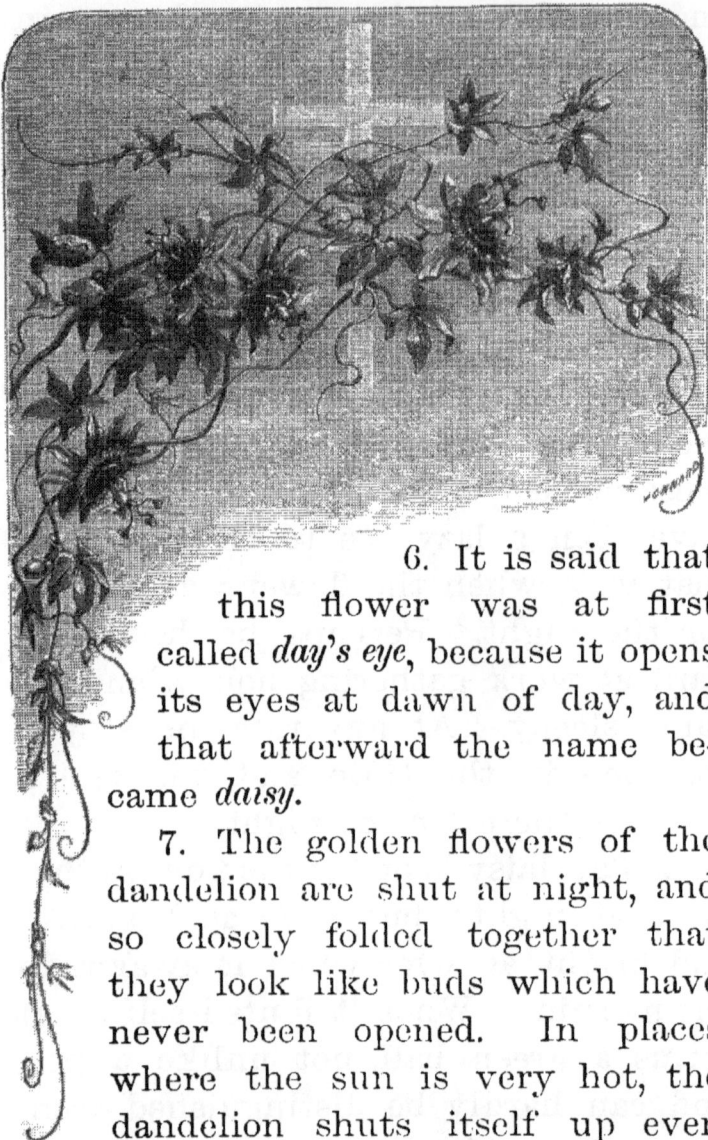

6. It is said that this flower was at first called *day's eye*, because it opens its eyes at dawn of day, and that afterward the name became *daisy*.

7. The golden flowers of the dandelion are shut at night, and so closely folded together that they look like buds which have never been opened. In places where the sun is very hot, the dandelion shuts itself up even during the day, and in this way is sheltered from the heat and kept from

8. Some flowers hang their heads at night, as if nodding in their sleep, but lift them again in the morning, to welcome the light. Others have a particular time to open. Some flowers, though open during the day, give out fragrance only when night comes on.

9. Flowers differ as much in size and form as in odor. One of the most remarkable in form is the passion flower, a native of South America. But little imagination is required to trace in this beautiful flower many of the emblems of our Lord's passion, as, for example, the crown of thorns, the nails, and the five wounds.

10. We read in the Bible that when Noe sent the dove a second time from the ark, it returned carrying an olive branch, which was accepted as a sign that the rain had ceased.

11. From that time, flowers have been used to represent certain qualities, conditions, and virtues ; as, for example, the olive branch is a symbol of peace; the laurel, of glory; the oak

passion flower, of religious fervor; the
sweet brier, of simplicity; the daisy,
of beauty and innocence; the rose-
mary, of remembrance; the hawthorn,
of hope; and the trumpet flower, of
fame. In fact, there is hardly a flower
that grows that has not some sentiment attached to it, in what is known
as the "language of flowers."

Language Lesson.

Write a short description of the flowers with
which you are familiar. Describe their appearance; tell whether they have a sweet odor or
are without fragrance; whether they grow wild
or are cultivated. In a word, write what you
know about flowers.

Explain the meaning of the following phrases:
"Every condition of life"; "cheer our pathway
in life"; "give out fragrance"; "little imagination is required"; "some sentiment attached
to it."

LESSON LXIX.

wĭĕld	tôrt'ûrĕ	ĭm'ple-ment
ġĕn'iŭs	re-strĭet'	ĭn'strṵ-ment
nŏs'tril	₩rôṵġḥt	mĭ'ero-seōpĕ
păs'sivĕ	tĕl'e-seōpĕ	hănd'i-erâfts'man

The Hand.

1. In many respects, the hand is the

The eye, the ear, and the nostril stand simply open: light, sound, and fragrance enter, and we are compelled to see, to hear, and to smell; but the hand selects what it shall touch, and touches what it pleases.

2. It puts away from it the things which it dislikes, and beckons toward it the things which it desires ; unlike the eye, which must often look on horrible sights from which it can not turn; and the ear, which can not escape from the torture of harsh, unpleasant sounds; and the nostril, which can not protect itself from offensive odors.

3. The hand cares not only for its own wants, but, when the organs of the other senses are rendered useless, takes their duties upon itself. The hand of the blind man goes with him as an eye through the streets, and safely guides him : it reads books for him, and helps to shorten the long hours.

4. The hand serves the deaf as willingly; and when the tongue is dumb and the ear closed, the fingers speak eloquently to the eye, and, by signs,

enable it to understand as well as if spoken words were used.

5. The organs of the other senses, also, are indebted to the hand for an increase of their powers. It constructs a telescope, a copy of the eye itself, with which to look upon the stars; and a microscope, another, but slightly different copy, which introduces the eye to a new world of wonders.

6. The hand constructs for the ear musical instruments to educate and delight it. It plucks for the nostril the flower which it longs to smell, and distils for it the fragrance which it covets. As for the tongue, if it had not the hand to serve it, it might give up its rights to be called the Lord of Taste. In short, the organ of touch is the instrument of the soul and the handmaid of its sister senses.

7. And if the hand thus generously serves the body, not less amply does it give expression to the genius and the wit, the courage and the affection, the will and the power of man. Put a sword into it, and it will fight for him;

put a plow into it, and it will till for him; put a harp into it, and it will play for him; put a pencil into it, and it will paint for him; put a pen into it, and it will speak for him, plead for him, pray for him.

8. What will it not do? What has it not done? A steam-engine is but a large hand, made to extend its powers by the little hand of man! An electric telegraph is but a long pen for that little hand to write with! All our huge cannons and other weapons of war, with which we slay our brethren, are only Cain's hand made bigger, and stronger, and bloodier!

9. What is a ship, a railway, a light-house, or a palace; what, indeed, is a whole city, all the cities of the globe, nay, the very globe itself, in so far as man has changed it, but the work of that giant hand, with which the human race, acting as one mighty man, has executed its will!

10. When I think of all that the human hand has wrought, from the

pluck the fruit of the forbidden tree, to that dark hour when the pierced hands of the Savior of the world were nailed to the cross, and of all that human hands have done of good and evil since, I lift up my hand and gaze upon it with wonder and awe. What an instrument for good it is! What an instrument for evil! And all the day long it is never idle.

11. There is no implement which the hand can not wield, and it should never in working hours be without one. We unwisely restrict the term "handicraftsman," or hand-worker, to the more laborious callings; but it belongs to all honest, earnest men and women, and is a title of which each should be proud.

12. For the king's hand there is the scepter, and for the soldier's hand the sword; for the carpenter's hand the saw, and for the smith's hand the hammer; for the farmer's hand the plow; for the miner's hand the spade; for the sailor's hand the oar; for the painter's

the chisel; for the poet's hand the pen; and for the woman's hand the needle.

Language Lesson.

1. What great difference is there between the organ of touch and the organs of the other senses? Illustrate this.
2. How does it take upon itself the duties of the eye? of the ear?
✸ 3. How does it increase the powers of the eye? of the ear?
4. To what does the hand give expression in man?
5. What may a steam-engine be considered? an electric telegraph? weapons of war?
6. To whom does the term *handicraftsman* properly apply?
7. What other words, or expressions, may be used for the following? "Features," "wrought," "implement," "restrict."

Familiar Talks on Common Things.

GOLD.—Why is gold such a precious metal? Gold is so precious because it is very rare and difficult to get; also because it is lasting and very beautiful.

For what else is gold remarkable? Gold is remarkable for being very ductile; that is, it may be drawn out into very fine wires, and beat into very thin leaves.

For what is gold-leaf used? Gold-leaf is used for gilding picture-frames, earthenware, the sides and edges of books, and many other things.

In what forms is gold found? Gold is found in dust, and in lumps called nuggets.

dust in the beds of rivers in Hungary, South America, and Africa.

Where is gold found in nuggets? Gold is found in nuggets in Russia, California, and Australia, mixed with a hard, flinty rock.

Are coins and jewelry made of pure gold? Coins and jewelry are not made of pure gold; by itself, gold would be too soft. It is hardened by mixing it with silver and copper. Such a mixture of two or more metals is called an *alloy*.

SILVER.—For what is silver remarkable? Silver is remarkable for its pure white color, and its brightness when polished.

For what else is silver remarkable? Silver is also remarkable because it can be drawn out into wires finer than the human hair, and beat into leaves.

Is silver-leaf as thin as gold-leaf? Silver-leaf is not as thin as gold-leaf; the thinnest leaf into which silver can be beaten is twice as thick as the thinnest gold-leaf.

In what state is silver when it is dug out of the earth? When silver is dug out of the earth, it is mixed with stones and dross.

What is a metal in that state called? A metal mixed with stones and other substances is called an ore.

How is the silver separated from the ore? Silver is extracted from the ore by melting.

Where are the greatest silver-mines? The greatest silver-mines are in Mexico and in Peru, South America; but silver is also found in the United States, and in Saxony, Hungary, Sweden, and Russia.

LEAD.—What kind of metal is lead? Lead is a soft, coarse, heavy metal, of a bluish-gray color.

For what is lead used? Lead is used for making water-pipes, lining cisterns, making bullets and small-shot, etc.

Where is lead found? Lead is found in large quantities in many parts of the United States and in Great Britain.

What are the chief alloys of lead? The chief alloys of lead are solder, a compound of lead and tin; and type-metal, a compound of lead and antimony.

IRON.—Why is iron so much used for manufacturing purposes? Iron is so much used for manufacturing purposes because it is very hard, is easily worked, and can bear a great strain.

Where is iron obtained? In the United States, iron is obtained in large quantities in Pennsylvania, Missouri, and Alabama.

What other mineral is generally found in the same districts? Coal, which is much required in smelting and manufacturing iron, is generally found in the same districts as that metal.

What are the principal kinds of iron? The principal kinds of iron are cast-iron, wrought-iron, and steel.

What is cast-iron? Cast-iron is iron melted and run into moulds. It is very hard and brittle.

For what is cast-iron used? Cast-iron is used for making grates, fenders, railings, and girders or beams used in building bridges, houses, etc.

How is wrought-iron made? Wrought-iron is made by passing a current of hot air through the iron while it is melting.

Wherein does wrought-iron differ from cast-iron? Wrought-iron is not brittle, but very tough; and it can be drawn out into wires and beaten into plates.

Can wrought-iron be melted? Wrought-iron can not be melted; but when red-hot it can be moulded by blows with a hammer, and punched with sharp tools.

For what is wrought-iron used? Wrought-iron is used in making rails for railways, horse-shoes, and other things made by the blacksmith.

How is steel made? Steel is made from wrought-iron, by heating it in charcoal, and beating it with heavy hammers.

For what is steel remarkable? Steel is finer and harder than wrought-iron; and may be made either brittle (as in pen-knives), or elastic (as in watch-springs).

What articles are made of steel? Knives, scissors, and sharp tools are made of steel.

What is a man who works in steel called? A man who works in steel is called a cutler, or maker of things that *cut*.

TIN. — What kind of a metal is tin? Tin is white, silvery, and easily bent.

For what is tin chiefly used? Tin is used for coating other metals.

Is it pure tin that the tinsmith uses? The tinsmith does not use pure tin; it is sheet-iron plated with tin.

What is tin-foil? Tin-foil is tin beat out into very thin leaves. Tin-foil is used for covering cakes of soap, chocolate, tobacco, etc.

Where are the principal tin-mines? The largest tin-mines are in Cornwall, England.

Into what alloys does tin enter? Tin enters into alloys of bronze, bell-metal, and solder.

Mention another alloy of tin very much used. Another alloy of tin is pewter, a compound of tin and a small quantity of lead.

Of what is the best pewter made? The best pewter is made of tin mixed with antimony and copper. It is calle 1 Britannia-metal, of which tea and coffee pots, as well as spoons, are often made.

ZINC. — What kind of a metal is zinc? Zinc is a bluish-white metal, bright when polished, and easily bent when rolled into sheets.

For what is zinc used? Zinc is used for roofing, baths, water-tanks, gutters, and the like; also in galvanic batteries, in engraving, and for galvanizing iron. It is largely used for making casts of statues, statuettes, and other ornamental castings.

MULTIPLICATION TABLE.

1 time 1 is 1	2 times 1 are 2	8 times 1 are 3
1 time 2 is 2	2 times 2 are 4	8 times 2 are 6
1 time 8 is 8	2 times 3 are 6	3 times 3 are 9
1 time 4 is 4	2 times 4 are 8	8 times 4 are 12
1 time 5 is 5	2 times 5 are 10	3 times 5 are 15
1 time 6 is 6	2 times 6 are 12	3 times 6 are 18
1 time 7 is 7	2 times 7 are 14	8 times 7 are 21
1 time 8 is 8	2 times 8 are 16	3 times 8 are 24
1 time 9 is 9	2 times 9 are 18	3 times 9 are 27
1 time 10 is 10	2 times 10 are 20	3 times 10 are 30
1 time 11 is 11	2 times 11 are 22	3 times 11 are 33
1 time 12 is 12	2 times 12 are 24	8 times 12 are 36

4 times 1 are 4	5 times 1 are 5	6 times 1 are 6
4 times 2 are 8	5 times 2 are 10	6 times 2 are 12
4 times 8 are 12	5 times 3 are 15	6 times 3 are 18
4 times 4 are 16	5 times 4 are 20	6 times 4 are 24
4 times 5 are 20	5 times 5 are 25	6 times 5 are 30
4 times 6 are 24	5 times 6 are 30	6 times 6 are 36
4 times 7 are 28	5 times 7 are 35	6 times 7 are 42
4 times 8 are 32	5 times 8 are 40	6 times 8 are 48
4 times 9 are 36	5 times 9 are 45	6 times 9 are 54
4 times 10 are 40	5 times 10 are 50	6 times 10 are 60
4 times 11 are 44	5 times 11 are 55	6 times 11 are 66
4 times 12 are 48	5 times 12 are 60	6 times 12 are 72

7 times 1 are 7	8 times 1 are 8	9 times 1 are 9
7 times 2 are 14	8 times 2 are 16	9 times 2 are 18
7 times 3 are 21	8 times 3 are 24	9 times 3 are 27
7 times 4 are 28	8 times 4 are 32	9 times 4 are 36
7 times 5 are 35	8 times 5 are 40	9 times 5 are 45
7 times 6 are 42	8 times 6 are 48	9 times 6 are 54
7 times 7 are 49	8 times 7 are 56	9 times 7 are 63
7 times 8 are 56	8 times 8 are 64	9 times 8 are 72
7 times 9 are 63	8 times 9 are 72	9 times 9 are 81
7 times 10 are 70	8 times 10 are 80	9 times 10 are 90
7 times 11 are 77	8 times 11 are 88	9 times 11 are 99
7 times 12 are 84	8 times 12 are 96	9 times 12 are 108

10 times 1 are 10	11 times 1 are 11	12 times 1 are 12
10 times 2 are 20	11 times 2 are 22	12 times 2 are 24
10 times 3 are 30	11 times 3 are 33	12 times 3 are 36
10 times 4 are 40	11 times 4 are 44	12 times 4 are 48
10 times 5 are 50	11 times 5 are 55	12 times 5 are 60
10 times 6 are 60	11 times 6 are 66	12 times 6 are 72
10 times 7 are 70	11 times 7 are 77	12 times 7 are 84
10 times 8 are 80	11 times 8 are 88	12 times 8 are 96
10 times 9 are 90	11 times 9 are 99	12 times 9 are 108
10 times 10 are 100	11 times 10 are 110	12 times 10 are 120
10 times 11 are 110	11 times 11 are 121	12 times 11 are 132
10 times 12 are 120	11 times 12 are 132	12 times 12 are 144

DIVISION TABLE.

1 in 1	1 time	2 in 2	1 time	3 in 3	1 time
1 in 2	2 times	2 in 4	2 times	3 in 6	2 times
1 in 3	3 times	2 in 6	3 times	3 in 9	3 times
1 in 4	4 times	2 in 8	4 times	3 in 12	4 times
1 in 5	5 times	2 in 10	5 times	3 in 15	5 times
1 in 6	6 times	2 in 12	6 times	3 in 18	6 times
1 in 7	7 times	2 in 14	7 times	3 in 21	7 times
1 in 8	8 times	2 in 16	8 times	3 in 24	8 times
1 in 9	9 times	2 in 18	9 times	3 in 27	9 times
1 in 10	10 times	2 in 20	10 times	3 in 30	10 times
1 in 11	11 times	2 in 22	11 times	3 in 33	11 times
1 in 12	12 times	2 in 24	12 times	3 in 36	12 times
4 in 4	1 time	5 in 5	1 time	6 in 6	1 time
4 in 8	2 times	5 in 10	2 times	6 in 12	2 times
4 in 12	3 times	5 in 15	3 times	6 in 18	3 times
4 in 16	4 times	5 in 20	4 times	6 in 24	4 times
4 in 20	5 times	5 in 25	5 times	6 in 30	5 times
4 in 24	6 times	5 in 30	6 times	6 in 36	6 times
4 in 28	7 times	5 in 35	7 times	6 in 42	7 times
4 in 32	8 times	5 in 40	8 times	6 in 48	8 times
4 in 36	9 times	5 in 45	9 times	6 in 54	9 times
4 in 40	10 times	5 in 50	10 times	6 in 60	10 times
4 in 44	11 times	5 in 55	11 times	6 in 66	11 times
4 in 48	12 times	5 in 60	12 times	6 in 72	12 times
7 in 7	1 time	8 in 8	1 time	9 in 9	1 time
7 in 14	2 times	8 in 16	2 times	9 in 18	2 times
7 in 21	3 times	8 in 24	3 times	9 in 27	3 times
7 in 28	4 times	8 in 32	4 times	9 in 36	4 times
7 in 35	5 times	8 in 40	5 times	9 in 45	5 times
7 in 42	6 times	8 in 48	6 times	9 in 54	6 times
7 in 49	7 times	8 in 56	7 times	9 in 63	7 times
7 in 56	8 times	8 in 64	8 times	9 in 72	8 times
7 in 63	9 times	8 in 72	9 times	9 in 81	9 times
7 in 70	10 times	8 in 80	10 times	9 in 90	10 times
7 in 77	11 times	8 in 88	11 times	9 in 99	11 times
7 in 84	12 times	8 in 96	12 times	9 in 108	12 times
10 in 10	1 time	11 in 11	1 time	12 in 12	1 time
10 in 20	2 times	11 in 22	2 times	12 in 24	2 times
10 in 30	3 times	11 in 33	3 times	12 in 36	3 times
10 in 40	4 times	11 in 44	4 times	12 in 48	4 times
10 in 50	5 times	11 in 55	5 times	12 in 60	5 times
10 in 60	6 times	11 in 66	6 times	12 in 72	6 times
10 in 70	7 times	11 in 77	7 times	12 in 84	7 times
10 in 80	8 times	11 in 88	8 times	12 in 96	8 times
10 in 90	9 times	11 in 99	9 times	12 in 108	9 times
10 in 100	10 times	11 in 110	10 times	12 in 120	10 times
10 in 110	mes		mes	12 in 132	11 times
10 in 120				12 in 144	12 times

www.ingramcontent.com/pod-product-compliance
Lightning Source LLC
Chambersburg PA
CBHW030358270326
41926CB00009B/1165